TREASURES OF THE WORLD

COLLECTION PLANNED AND DIRECTED BY

ALBERT SKIRA

TREASURES
OF
SPAIN

FROM CHARLES V TO GOYA

INTRODUCTION BY
F. J. SÁNCHEZ CANTÓN
Director of the Prado, Madrid

TEXT BY
ALEXANDRE CIRICI-PELLICER
of the University of Barcelona

SKIRA

Translated from the Spanish by Robin Kemball (Introduction),
Gladys Ronkin (Part 1) and Catherine Moran (Parts 2 and 3).

★

© 1965 by Editions d'Art Albert Skira, Geneva
Library of Congress Catalog Card Number: 65-24418

★

PRINTED IN SWITZERLAND

CONTENTS

LIST OF ILLUSTRATIONS

PART THREE

INTRODUCTION

Users of this book, whether they read the text in detail, consult its pages for reference, or content themselves with admiring the fine illustrations it contains, will doubtless be glad of an introductory sketch outlining the distinctive characteristics of Spanish art from the Renaissance to the present century. It will first be necessary, however, to summarize very briefly some five centuries of Spanish history.

The diversity of her soil and climate, the broken contours of her relief, her situation in the extreme southwestern corner of Europe—all these factors played a part in shaping Spain's destiny in ancient and medieval times. The domination of her original inhabitants by Celts, Phoenicians, Carthaginians, Romans, Byzantines, Visigoths, and Moors in turn determined the checkered pattern of her evolution through the twenty centuries of her history described in another volume of this series.

At the time when the works of art described in the present volume were beginning to make their appearance, the historical and political situation in the Iberian peninsula was, very briefly, as follows: (1) The greater part of Spanish territory was ruled by Isabella I of Castile and Ferdinand II of Aragon; the most pressing task facing these two sovereigns, who had married in 1469, was the reduction and conquest of the kingdom of Granada, the last stronghold of Moorish power in Spain—this was achieved in 1492. (2) In the west of the Peninsula, the Kingdom of Portugal was at the height of its power, with Portuguese expansion and colonization in Africa and Asia proceeding apace. (3) Under the protection of the "Catholic Queen" came the first stages in the discovery of America and the conversion of its peoples to Christianity.

The untimely death, in 1497, of the Crown Prince, Don Juan, interfered with the normal processes of succession. The throne now devolved upon the prince's eldest sister, Isabella, who was married to Manuel I of Portugal. Their son, Dom Miguel, who, had he succeeded, would have united the whole Peninsula under one head, died in infancy. As the result of a continued series of misfortunes, the crown of the "Catholic Sovereigns" (as Ferdinand and Isabella came to be called) ultimately passed to their grandson Charles, who had been born in Ghent, the son of their second daughter, Joanna the Mad, and of Philip the Handsome of Burgundy, who was the son and heir of the German Emperor Maximilian I. On the death of the latter in 1519, Charles—who was already Charles I of Spain—also succeeded to the Imperial crown as Charles V (by which title he is usually known). With this, Spain became increasingly involved in European affairs, expending in the process energies which she dearly needed elsewhere, in order to accomplish her mission in America and in Asia, where the conversion of the Philippines to Christianity had by now extended her sphere of vital interests. In this way, Spain, from having been a political "extremity," suddenly found herself cast in a central role in European and, indeed, in world affairs. But the apparent greatness thrust upon her was an illusory one, in no way consonant with her true internal strength. In fact, barely recovered from the centuries-old struggle against the Moors and bled white by expeditions overseas, Spain at this time resembled rather some undernourished Colossus.

Charles V, who understood the true situation clearly, decided to divide the lands over which he held sway, giving the territory of the crowns of Castile and Aragon to his son, the future Philip II, and his German possessions to his brother Ferdinand. But between these two new States lay Naples, Sicily, the Duchy of Milan, and Flanders. The bold stroke of marrying Philip to Mary Tudor of England (1554) failed to achieve the desired result, the latter failing to bear him a son to succeed him. Nevertheless, without entering here into unnecessary detail, it is fair to say that the spiritual force derived from her firmly welded religious unity in fact actuated and guided developments in Spain, until the accession of Philip IV (1621-1665) ushered in that series of military reverses which was later to assume disastrous proportions under his weak and luckless son, Charles II (1665-1700). The unity of the Peninsula, achieved by the incorporation of Portugal in 1580, was to prove short-lived, lasting only until 1640, when, after several insurrections, Portugal regained her independence.

During the two centuries just referred to, the arts in Spain developed with astounding vigor and amplitude, thanks in large measure to the fine taste and expert knowledge in this domain displayed by successive Spanish rulers: Isabella the Catholic, Charles V, Philip II, III, and IV were all devotees of fine painting and grandiose architecture. Indeed, both Philip II and his grandson, Philip IV, may fairly be regarded as veritable connoisseurs of the arts. Most of the plates reproduced in this book could, in fact, well be classified according to the Spanish monarchs reigning at the time they were produced. Even the feeble and deformed Charles II, the last member of the House of Austria to occupy the Spanish throne, appreciated good painting and could boast of considerable knowledge in this domain.

The eighteenth century witnessed the advent of a new dynasty, the Bourbons. Charles II was succeeded by Philip V, great-grandson of Philip IV. By now, Spain's once leading role in European affairs was in the descendant and—as if shorn of her creative potential generally—she became little more than a satellite of France in the field of letters and the arts also. Various factors combined, as the century advanced, to free her from this humiliating state of dependence. Chief among these was the fact that Spanish kings like Ferdinand VI, Charles III, and Charles IV proved to be no less enthusiastic lovers of the arts than their Austrian forebears.

A rapid survey of the reigns just mentioned will make it easier for the reader to understand the evolution of architecture and sculpture in Spain. Under Ferdinand and Isabella (1479-1516), in the period between the Middle Ages and the Renaissance, building proceeded in the Late Gothic style, influenced by technical and decorative devices of Moorish origin; in addition, certain features borrowed from Italy began to make their appearance. Flemish, German, and Spanish artists were invited to the Spanish Court and paintings were bought—especially by Isabella—from Flanders and, to a lesser extent, from Italy.

Charles V's reign (1516-1556) witnessed the construction of buildings, secular and religious, in the style of the now triumphant Renaissance. Charles commissioned paintings from Titian, who was to exercise a decisive influence on the subsequent development of Spanish painting. At the same time, Italian painters were invited to Spain, while several Spaniards went to study the arts in Italy.

Philip II (1556-1598) was a regular patron of Titian, though the latter never actually came to Spain. In the course of his travels through Italy, Flanders, Lower Germany, and England, Philip developed at once a remarkably fine yet varied taste, appreciating widely differing schools and techniques and acquiring as a result a notable selection of works, ranging from early Flemish paintings to others by such advanced Venetians as Veronese, Tintoretto, and Bassano. He even patronized Mannerist painters, who at that time represented the *avant-garde*. For the supreme monument of his reign, the Escorial, he employed both Spaniards and Italians, displaying remarkable judgment in his assessment of their work. This monument effectively symbolizes the grandeur of the Renaissance style in its final phase.

Philip III (1598-1621) followed in the tradition of his father, though with less dedication of purpose and less critical acumen. It was he who received the first painters associated with the use of *tenebroso* contrasts, and in 1603 Rubens even painted at the Spanish Court for a period of eight months or so. It was during this reign that the art of carving in polychrome wood reached such splendid heights, thanks to artists like Gregorio Fernández and the pupils of Pompeo Leoni, in Castile, and also to the Andalusian schools.

Philip IV (1621-1665), who commissioned buildings in Baroque style, was also passionately fond of fine paintings, and was, in fact, a friend of Velázquez for nearly forty years. He had Rubens at his Court in 1628-1629 and, when the latter returned to Antwerp, ordered dozens of canvases from him. He bought pictures in Italy, in Flanders, and in England, amassing a fantastic number of masterpieces in the palaces of Madrid, the Buen Retiro, the Pardo, and the Escorial. From the palace inventories, we know that in 1700 the Spanish Crown possessed no less than 5,539 pictures!

Philip V (1700-1746), the first of the Spanish Bourbons, summoned French sculptors for the fountains in the gardens of La Granja, his palace near Segovia; he also engaged French artists as portrait painters at his Court. Together with his second wife, Elizabeth Farnese, he organized the recovery and restoration of many of the pictures damaged in the great fire which destroyed the Alcázar in Madrid in 1734, and initiated the construction of a new palace there.

Ferdinand VI (1746-1759) continued the work of rebuilding this palace, engaging painters and sculptors from Italy for this purpose. It was he, too, who took the momentous step of founding the Spanish Royal Academy of Fine Arts.

Charles III (1759-1788), who arrived in Spain in 1759, having ruled the Kingdom of the Two Sicilies since 1734, not only transformed the face of Madrid; for the redecoration of the palace ceilings, he commissioned the two most eminent painters of the time—Anton Raphael Mengs, the Romanized German, and Giovanni Battista Tiepolo, last of the great Venetian fresco painters. These two lent a new impetus to the arts in Spain and, with the help of the teaching and support given by the Academy, restored them to their former position of splendor. One name is sufficient to demonstrate this: Francisco de Goya.

Before his accession, Charles IV (1788-1808) had already established a fine collection of pictures by various painters, among whom Goya was his favorite. With the French occupation (1808-1813) and the losses occasioned by the Napoleonic wars, the arts in Spain underwent a temporary eclipse, but this happily proved to be of brief duration. With the restoration of the Bourbon Ferdinand VII (1814-1833), building—now based on Neoclassical norms—was resumed on a wide scale. It was on Ferdinand's initiative, likewise, that the famous Prado Museum was turned into a picture gallery. Hung with magnificent paintings hitherto housed in the various royal palaces, this building was finally opened to the public on November 19th, 1819, and so virtually inaugurates the nineteenth century.

The period of unrest which followed—marked by the struggle for independence of the Spanish-American colonies, civil war, revolution, the Republic, etc.—produced a Romantic school of painters of remarkable quality. To these were added, in the later decades, history painters, landscape artists, and portrait painters of vigorous personality. The Prado Museum increased its store of treasures, thanks to the supply of paintings from the Escorial, decreed by Isabella II (1833-1868), and to the incorporation of the so-called National Museum of Painting and Sculpture, containing works of art taken from the monasteries which had been suppressed.

If any proof were needed of the vitality of Spanish art in the present century, it would be enough to list such names as Gaudí in architecture, Sorolla, Zuloaga, Solana, Picasso, and Dalí in painting, and Julio Antonio, Mateo Hernández, and José Capuz in sculpture—to mention only a few examples of diverse trends, without attempting to assign first place to any particular artist.

There may well be readers who will ask: "What are the guiding aesthetic theories and technical principles that have influenced the development of the fine arts in Spain in the modern and contemporary era?" A full reply to this question would far exceed the scope of this introductory survey; the most that can be attempted here is to provide the reader with a few brief indications.

As was only natural, the first signs of Renaissance influence made their way into Spain through Aragon, with the twelve reliefs carved between 1417 and 1424 for the retrochoir of Valencia Cathedral by Giuliano Poggibonsi, a Florentine sculptor whose work in some ways echoes the style of Ghiberti. Twenty years later, Nicolao Florentino painted his fresco of the *Last Judgment* in the apse of Salamanca Cathedral; also by his hand are the fifty-four pictures on the altarpiece, all imbued with typical Renaissance features. However, these examples of the new style, like the vault in Valencia, his native city, executed by Jacomart, a painter employed at the Neapolitan court of Alfonso V, of the House of Aragon, or the arrival of manuscripts illuminated in the new style in Italy, must be recognized for what they in fact were—imported works, or works by foreign artists.

Indisputably Spanish, by contrast, are those works of art promoted by eminent personalities of the time, especially by members of the Mendoza family, such as the second Count of Tendilla and his uncle, Cardinal Don Pedro González de Mendoza, who were responsible for fine buildings in Valladolid (Colegio de Santa Cruz, 1490) and in Mondéjar (San Antonio, 1487-1509), or the Duke of Medinaceli (Palace of Cogolludo, 1492-1495). Other monuments betray the growing influence of the new Italian style. Certain architectonic devices and decorative motifs had to be imported, since no Spanish text-books were yet available from which to learn them.

In the sphere of literature, the influence of the Renaissance had been more direct and more widespread; we have only to recall the "sonnets in the Italian mode" of the Marquis of Santillana, the father of Cardinal Mendoza himself. To find an authentic

Spanish treatise on art, we have to wait until 1526, the year which saw the publication in Toledo of a work entitled *Medidas del Romano* (Proportions of the Roman Style), written by Diego de Sagreda and published at the expense of one Don Alonso de Fonseca, Archbishop of Toledo, a Maecenas whose family played a part in the patronage of the arts comparable to that of the Mendozas. Not only was this the first work on ancient architecture to be written outside Italy; its translation into French in 1539 even anticipated French publications of the kind.

Using the dialogue form fashionable at that time, the author formulates his Purist standards, discussing "the proportions which craftsmen desirous of imitating... Roman edifices must know, for the lack of which they have committed, and each day continue committing, many errors of malproportion and unsightliness in the formation of bases and capitals." For the first time in Spanish, we here find mention of two artists who were then at the peak of their powers—Felipe Bigarny, the sculptor, and Cristóbal de Andino, a metal-worker who specialized in wrought-iron altar screens. In the dialogue, the painter León Picardo acts as interlocutor. However, as we shall see, the rigid theories here expounded were ill suited to the idiosyncrasies of the Spanish temperament; even so, the fact that this work went through at least four more editions in the course of the sixteenth century is proof enough that it was widely read and circulated.

Though devoid of all technical matter, the work by Cristóbal de Villalón, published in Valladolid in 1539 under the title *Ingeniosa comparación entre lo antiguo y lo presente* (Ingenious Comparison between the Ancient and Modern Styles), is interesting for the highly credible account the author renders of the discussions in which he became involved concerning his artistic and humanistic criteria. Like Sagreda before him, Villalón also makes use of the dialogue form in order to develop his theme. In this connection, the term "ancient" must be understood as including only the pure Classical school, while "modern" also includes Gothic, in reference to which the author extols the cathedrals of Toledo, León, and Seville, citing also San Pablo in Valladolid, and the most recent buildings of the Colegio de Santa Cruz in the same city, the Hospital Real in Santiago de Compostela, etc. More incisively than Sagreda, Villalón bestows praise on numerous contemporary artists and on others who had only recently died: Raphael, Dürer, Michelangelo, Bandinelli, Giulio de Aquiles, Alessandro Mayner, Alonso Berruguete, Felipe Bigarny, Gil de Siloe, Cristóbal de Andino, the Villalpandos and the armorers, Salvador and Colman; finally, without actually naming Enrique de Arfe, he declares that his monstrances in León, Cordova, and Toledo have no equal. The author gives the impression of being unaware that the artists he mentions, with the exception of the last-named, strove to recreate and believed that they were in fact recreating the beauties of Antiquity; they were most definitely artists of the Renaissance, and not mere continuers of the Gothic tradition—though it is true that artists like Berruguete, Gil de Siloe, and Bigarny had their roots in that tradition.

Of considerable importance for an understanding of the ideas on art prevalent in Spain at that time are various works which remained unpublished, and so cannot have exercised any widespread influence, though they may well have been known in certain studios and have been circulated by means of handwritten copies. These include the *Diálogos de la Pintura* (Dialogues on Painting), originally written in Portuguese by the miniaturist Francisco de Holanda (1538), and later done into Spanish (1563) by the painter Manuel Denis—of particular importance for the various expressions of opinion attributed to Michelangelo; the *Comentarios de la Pintura* (Commentaries on Painting), by Felipe de Guevara (1560?); and the prologue to the Spanish translation of Vitruvius, which contains numerous data not included in the version published in 1569 and ascribed to Miguel de Urrea, although the true author is mentioned in the original manuscript, which has been preserved; this was Lázaro de Velasco, a priest and architect from Granada, and the son of Jacopo Florentino, himself a sculptor and architect. Velasco's work is of importance for another reason: the introduction which he appended to the text supplies valuable information concerning architecture in Granada at the time he wrote. Another work which remained unpublished was *De las estatuas antiguas* (Concerning Ancient Statues), by Diego de Villalta (1590), the only treatise exclusively devoted to sculpture; it also dealt with contemporary sculptors, mentioning certain works of Michelangelo. The same book includes a reference to an *Arte de la Pintura* (Art of Painting) written by Fernando de Avila, a painter at the court of Philip II; this latter work is known to us only by this reference and by the list of biographies of fourteen painters, the finest of those working in Castile during the sixteenth century, if we except Pedro Machuca and El Greco, whom, however, the author also knew. The loss of this work is undoubtedly the most serious one suffered in the bibliography of Spanish art.

Works which did appear in print, and so enjoyed a considerable circulation, include the *Tercero y cuarto libro de Arquitectura de Sebastián Serlio* (Third and Fourth Book on Architecture by Sebastiano Serlio), translated into Spanish by another architect, Francisco de Villalpando. Originally published in Toledo in 1552, this work—an outstanding source of information on the Renaissance in Spain—met with such success that it was republished the following year and again in 1574. Another work which went through several editions in the course of the seventeenth and eighteenth centuries was a practical manual entitled *De varia conmensuración para la Escultura y Arquitectura* (Concerning Various Methods of Commensuration in Sculpture and Architecture). Originally printed in Seville in 1585, it was the work of Juan de Arfe y Villafañe, known as the "sculptor in gold and silver." Juan was the grandson of the Enrique de Arfe mentioned earlier, and the son of Antonio, another great silversmith, who belonged to the Plateresque school, just as Enrique belonged to the Gothic, while Juan followed the pure Renaissance style. Juan's book contains comments and instructions in verse form, to help the reader memorize them—a device which greatly enhances its instructional value; at the same time, it also contains useful historical data.

The sixteenth century closes with the descriptive and critical study of the Escorial, *La fundación de San Lorenzo el Real*, by Friar José de Sigüenza, forming the third part of his *Historia de la Orden de San Jerónimo* (History of the Order of St Jerome); although not published until 1605, this volume was in fact completed on September 21st, 1602. The author, an Hieronymite monk and the leading connoisseur of Spanish art of his day, combined extreme purity with wide catholicity of taste, admiring as he did the early Flemish painters, those of the Venetian school, and others from Rome and from Florence; with acute perception, he decried the idiosyncrasies of the Mannerists, exposing them to merciless and penetrating criticism. Perhaps his only shortcoming as a critic was his failure to appreciate El Greco. Sigüenza's work is of tremendous value for a proper understanding of the evolution of the arts in Spain during his own century and the one which followed.

The studies by Gutiérrez de los Ríos (1600) and by Don Juan de Butrón (1626), as well as one or two others, deal mostly with the rights and privileges of artists, rather than with their productions, ideas, or techniques. Similarly, the writings of Pablo de Céspedes (1604), the Mannerist painter, call for no comment here.

Two painters whose views were in many respects diametrically opposed, Vincenzo Carducci (in Spanish, Vincencio Carducho, for he left his native Florence at the age of nine) and Francisco Pacheco (1564-1654), an Andalusian, each produced books of the utmost value for an understanding of the theory and history of Spanish painting during its golden age.

Pacheco took the lead in including, in his *Descripción de verdaderos retratos de ilustres y memorables varones* (Description of Authentic Portraits of Illustrious and Noteworthy Gentlemen), begun in 1599, portraits of three painters—Céspedes, Luis de Vargas, and Pedro de Campaña (or Pieter Kempeneer)—together with biographical sketches of each. According to the account given in the *Arte de la Pintura*, this work was never completed and remained unpublished.

As for Carducho, in 1633 he published his *Diálogos de la Pintura* (Dialogues on Painting), a learned treatise describing works of art he had seen in the course of a long journey through Italy, Flanders, and France, as well as other works included in Spanish collections, both public and private. In this account, he censured Velázquez (of whom he was intensely jealous), though without actually naming him, and castigated the new dramatic realism, although several of his own works show definite traces of naturalistic influence.

Pacheco's *Arte de la Pintura*—not published until 1649, but in fact completed over ten years before this, on January 24th, 1638—would seem to have been called forth by Carducho's book, to which it appears to be a closely reasoned reply. Though referring to Carducho as his "close friend," Pacheco repeatedly, and quite justifiably, goes out of his way to praise Velázquez (who was both his pupil and his son-in-law), taking up the defense of various portraits and still lifes which Carducho had attacked in his *Diálogos de la Pintura*.

Compared with Pacheco's great work, the *Discursos practicables del nobilísimo arte de la Pintura* (Practical Discourses on the Most Noble Art of Painting) of Jusepe Martínez—an Aragonese painter and friend of Velázquez—is lacking in relief, despite the wealth of anecdotes it contains. The book was written around 1673, but did not appear in print until the nineteenth century. A strange treatise is that called *Pintura sabia* (Learned Painting), written by the painter and Benedictine friar, Juan Ricci, or Rizi, and only published in 1930. This work, in which the author invented the "Solomonic order" in architecture, is of value less for its text than for the various sketches of the nude which it contains, including several female nudes. Other works deserving only brief mention here are those by Vicente Salvador y Gómez, Félix Lucio de Espinosa, and José García Hidalgo (1691).

In architecture, we find a work of technical character, the *Arte y uso de Arquitectura* (Art and Usage in Architecture) published in 1663 by an Augustinian friar, Lorenzo de San Nicolás, who added his own autobiography. Less useful, on account of its frequent erudite digressions, is the *Excelencias de la Arquitectura* (Excellences of Architecture) of Domingo de Andrade, the great Baroque architect of Santiago de Compostela; it appeared in 1695.

In the field of painting, no other treatise approaches in importance the veritable encyclopedia produced by Antonio Palomino y Velasco, *El Museo pictórico y Escala óptica de la Pintura* (The Pictorial Museum and Optical Scale of Painting), published in three volumes between 1715 and 1724. The third of these, *El Parnaso español pintoresco laureado* (The Spanish Collection of Eminent Painters), contains 226 biographical studies of Spanish sculptors and painters, as well as some non-Spanish artists who had at one time been in the service of the Kings and Queens of Spain, including Titian, Anthonis Mor (Antonio Moro), and Luca Giordano. The work includes artists from 1500 onwards. The wide range of tastes catered for and the wealth of information provided place this work in a class of its own among Spanish writings of this kind. Himself a follower of the Baroque school, Palomino recognized the merits of the Primitives, such as Fernando Gallego, was a great admirer of Titian, and even of the Mannerists, and bestowed generous praise on the Realist school, including some of its younger and less famous members.

As the eighteenth century advanced, important works appearing included the publications of the Royal Academy of Fine Arts (beginning in 1752), notably the papers read there by Jovellanos, and the writings of Preciado de la Vega, Mengs, Ponz,

Bosarte, Mayans, Llaguno, and Ceán Bermúdez. Detailed examination of these would far exceed the limits set by the present survey, but they are mentioned here to enable the reader to seek out those details that are of particular interest to him.

Having very briefly reviewed the relevant texts and historical data, we may now take a glance at the more outstanding, or more decisive, characteristics of Spanish art during the period from the sixteenth to the twentieth century. Perhaps its most striking general characteristic throughout this period, as indeed in earlier periods, is an inborn tensile force, an overflowing vigor and vitality. Spanish art may attract some, repel others; it never leaves the spectator indifferent. He will look in vain for complexity of thought or academic exactitude, but he cannot fail to be moved by the emotional force, the depth of feeling, which pervade these works.

Even in those works influenced by the Renaissance and Neoclassical styles, with their essentially "disciplined" nature, one still detects certain rebellious minds. A few examples will suffice to confirm this. Alonso Berruguete, the greatest Spanish sculptor of the sixteenth century, who spent part of his youth in Italy and watched Michelangelo at work, introduced poses and gestures in his statues which, though inspired by memories of that great master, yet betray an unmistakably and fundamentally Gothic temperament. El Greco, for all that he hailed from Venice and belonged to the Mannerist school, later rode roughshod over the tenets of the Italian school, settled down in Toledo, adopted Spanish ways and customs, and produced canvases imbued with a brand of spiritual asceticism, introducing innovations in his colors, which he made cold on some occasions, but warm, sumptuous, even Oriental, on others. Juan de Juní, another sculptor, born in France and also a Mannerist after his fashion, later touched heights of impassioned realism; while Gregorio Fernández, born in Galicia— devoutly religious but withal a realist—was a master in creating seductive skin texture, modeling the flesh of his religious effigies with inimitable delicacy and displaying a sensitivity which one would never have expected to find in the rough and ready Castilian milieu in which he worked. And so, finally, to the classic example of the great artist in revolt against the Academy and its norms—Francisco de Goya.

From what has been said, the reader will infer that the Baroque style found a propitious soil and climate in Spain simply because the seventeenth century with which it coincided, although an age of political and military decline, happened also to be the golden age of Spanish painting and sculpture. This century was dominated by a type of "artistic realism" which might be qualified as "whole," or "integral," inasmuch as fidelity in interpretation was not confined to the physical, but also extended to the spiritual sphere—which is, of course, no less "real" a part of man. In consequence, the school known generally as "Spanish realism" was something far more than mere "naturalism," recognizing as it did the bond between, and interpenetration of, the spiritual and the natural.

While it is true that religious beliefs were the main source of inspiration for Spanish artists during the period under review, this does not mean that celestial scenes or mystical-ecstatic visions were not portrayed in such a manner as to render them at once credible and comprehensible. Some years ago, I pointed out how the greatest religious painters—Ribera, Zurbarán, Murillo—portrayed the appearances of Christ and of the Virgin Mary to the servants of God as if apprehended by the latter in their dreams, citing in illustration *Jacob's Dream* by Ribera, Zurbarán's *Vision of St Peter Nolasco*, and Murillo's *Dream of the Roman Knight*. This essentially Spanish approach is likewise confirmed by the habit of depicting the favor of heaven as being received by way of a vision—as, for instance, in Zurbarán's *Vision of St Alonso Rodríguez*, in which it is the spiritual rather than the physical eyes which perceive.

Another peculiarity of the Spanish realists is the keen sense of the comic, at times extending to the burlesque, which they display when handling mythological themes, in sharp contrast to the more stylized, poetic, and serious approach we find in Italy, France, and Flanders. Examples from Velázquez, Ribera, and Carreño immediately spring to mind. In this respect, Spanish painting goes hand in hand with Spanish literature: Góngora, Lope de Vega, and Quevedo do not hesitate to poke fun—at times gracefully, wittily, at others bluntly, cruelly—at the heathen gods.

There is a certain link between this disrespectful strain inherent in the Spanish national genius and another peculiarity found in Spanish painting and sculpture—namely, its predilection for the popular, and even the vulgar. When treating religious themes, Spanish artists tend to cling to traditional, popular interpretations of events, rather than follow the accounts handed down by the mystics. This clearly defined trend is reinforced, from the early seventeenth century onwards, by the large numbers of pictures which portray figures from the common people, in interiors or out of doors, by painters such as Loarte, Puga, Antolínez, Murillo, Villavicencio, and including also the early works of Ribera and Velázquez. Moreover, it should be noted that such scenes are not mere genre paintings in the manner of, say, a Teniers, but are genuine portraits, the subjects of which are accorded exactly the same treatment as if they had been nobles. Parallel with this trend is the tradition whereby Spanish portraitists depict clowns and jesters in sympathetic fashion; it was something more than mere compliance with the demands of court etiquette which impelled Moro, Sánchez Coello, Pantoja de la Cruz, Liaño, Carreño, and Francisco Rizi to portray dwarfs and lunatics, the playthings of kings and queens. As for Velázquez, he painted no less than a dozen or so of these "palace vermin" at the very peak of his career. The same taste for popular themes is clearly brought out in further paintings by this great artist and in others by his son-in-law, Mazo; these include the hunting scenes and the magnificent *View of Saragossa*, which depicts the solemn entry into the city of Philip IV and the Crown Prince, whom one barely notices, while the people, represented by all the different classes, line the bank of the river.

This popular trend became even more marked during the eighteenth century, when the founding of the Royal Tapestry Factory entailed the commissioning of hundreds of cartoons painted in oils on canvas, depicting scenes from the everyday life of the people—*fiestas*, games, brawls, peasant life, crowded markets, and even accidents at work—all designed to decorate the royal palaces with scenes depicted in their natural surroundings, mostly in Madrid and its environs.

In case it should be thought that popular themes such as these found no expression in sculpture, it would be sufficient to mention the widespread popularity of Nativity *crèches* containing numerous figures modeled in clay or wood, and arranged in groups to represent a variety of episodes from the story of our Lord's birth. The national taste for lavish ornamentation being what it was, such figures were used in eighteenth-century Spain to people legendary Nativity scenes with highly realistic reproductions of peasants, shepherds, soldiers, etc.

The popular trend in sculpture also found expression in the polychrome statues—more particularly those depicting Christ's Passion—designed to be carried in the Holy Week processions. From the early seventeenth century onwards, this tradition provides one of the profoundest and most shining illustrations of the Spanish religious soul. Artistic and religious centers sprang up in Valladolid, Andalusia, and Murcia, to mention only the leading names. In this particular type of statuary—generally wooden figures of divine or saintly personages, carved in the round and then painted in bright colors—Spanish sculpture is unique.

Reference has already been made to the Spanish propensity for the ornate—despite the solemnity which is generally considered to be the most distinctive feature of national taste. This wealth of ornamentation lent an added splendor to the two most specifically Spanish phases in architecture during the period covered by the present volume, the styles known as Plateresque and Churrigueresque respectively. In the former, which evolved during the first third of the sixteenth century, these ornate elements, of Italian inspiration, were as a rule applied to structures fundamentally Gothic, though in some cases also Moorish, in style. The second school, which flourished during the late seventeenth and early eighteenth centuries, owed its name to its most gifted architect, José de Churriguera, though the term has since taken on a somewhat derogatory connotation, as have at one time or another such terms as Gothic, Baroque, and Rococo. Today, when the academic norms and conventions of former times have themselves become outmoded, it is fair to say that the decorative power inherent in the Churrigueresque style is appreciated at its just value. The intense exuberance once imputed to secular and religious architecture in Andalusia and Eastern Spain is also found in no less marked degree in Castile, León, and Galicia. Though these regions are usually regarded as altogether quieter and more sober in style, their Late Plateresque and Baroque periods are in fact no less flamboyant.

To conclude this introductory survey, a word or two on one aspect of Spanish art which cannot fail to have struck the reader—the presence, in widely differing epochs of its history, of foreign artists in the Peninsula, many of whom with time became authentic exponents of the Spanish tradition. This phenomenon is explained by the rapid and thorough assimilation of such figures as the German Colonia family (who worked in Burgos); Siloe and Bigarny (also active in Burgos, though the former hailed from Antwerp and the latter from Burgundy); Juan Guas, a Frenchman whose real name was probably spelt Houasse, who worked in Toledo, as did Enrique de Egas, who came from Brussels; Juan de Juní, another Frenchman (probably from Joigny, in Champagne), who was active in Oporto and Valladolid; Pietro Torrigiani and Jacopo Florentino (or L'Indaco), both Florentines, who settled in Seville and in Granada respectively; and—overshadowing all of these—the towering figure of Domenicos Theotocopulos, called El Greco. It seems likely that all these men were already trained artists by the time they reached Spain, but they acclimatized themselves so well to their land of adoption that all may be regarded as unquestionable and authentic representatives of the Spanish tradition. The genius of a Colonia and a Guas enabled them to make use of certain solutions previously adopted by Moorish architects; in so doing, however, they avoided any slavish imitation of form, penetrating rather to the essential and technical aspects of the work of their models. Jacopo Florentino and Juan de Juní carved in the manner of the realist school, of whom they may be considered fellow-representatives, or rivals; but since, in their turn, they had to serve as models for others coming after them, they forsook the compact texture of the Realists, without, however, entirely discarding it. This process of assimilation—presenting its own characteristic features—was so successfully accomplished that it made an essential contribution to the ultimate triumph of native art and artists in Spain.

F. J. Sánchez Cantón
Madrid, June 1965

1

THE SPLENDOR
OF THE CONQUERORS

TITIAN (1477-1576). EQUESTRIAN PORTRAIT OF THE EMPEROR CHARLES V AT THE BATTLE OF MÜHLBERG, DETAIL. 1548. PRADO, MADRID.

THE SPAIN OF CHARLES V

Spain was the first European power to take on world dimensions: this was the outstanding feature of her history between the reign of Charles V and the age of Goya and made of it a great, unique adventure.

When America was discovered, Spain did not yet exist as a unified State—more than two centuries were to elapse before it came into being. The two most powerful kingdoms of the Peninsula, Castile and Aragon, were linked only by a tenuous dynastic marriage, that of Ferdinand and Isabella, whose joint reign began in 1479; and after the death of Queen Isabella (1504) even this link was broken.

The fabulous heritage of the Emperor Charles V was made up of Castile and its American possessions, the states of the Crown of Aragon (Aragon, Catalonia, Valencia, Majorca, Naples, Sicily and Sardinia), the territories inherited from Mary of Burgundy (the Low Countries, Artois and Franche-Comté), besides the family domains in Austria. What was to be called Spain was united for the first time under one crown, although until the eighteenth century it continued to be nothing more than a juxtaposition of countries separated by radical economic, social, political and military differences and divided from each other by frontiers and customs duties which frequently led to violent disputes. Yet in some ways there was a sort of balance to offset the differences in their respective positions. Castile, with 7,000,000 inhabitants, was the most heavily populated state, while tiny Catalonia, with only 300,000 inhabitants, had the advantage of being the political center of the Kingdom of Aragon, the leading confederation of states in all of Charles V's dominions, as the Emperor himself recognized in the Cortes of Catalonia in 1519.

These two states, Castile and Catalonia, were the springboards for Charles V's twofold maritime action: Castile, facing the Atlantic, for the great American adventure; and Catalonia, facing the Mediterranean, for the Italian and African ventures.

Charles V's role in history was not a national one, by any means. His territories were often at war because of international interests and problems—against France, for example—or involved in the internal struggles of the German Empire. At other times they fought from special motives, as when the Castilians went to America in search of riches, or when the Catalonians waged war to preserve the traditional market for their textiles in their own Italian territories or to open up new markets in Castile, Portugal, Africa and the Americas. The empire of Charles V was a territorial and military power which, it has been aptly said, had "feet of clay," a rickety foundation and a disorganized economy.

This brief historical sketch can help us to understand the nature of the power-center established by Charles V: extremely dynamic, but by no means solid. There was a certain unity in the various undertakings, but on an international basis of dynastic origin, without any common ethnic or economic interests. Spanish policy was characterized by shifting outlines in its historical development and in the extension of its influence. The government of the country was more an association of men of initiative and adventurers than an organized state, which after all did not exist.

True popular mass movements in sixteenth-century Spain, the rising of the communes in Castile and the "Germania" factions in Valencia and Aragon, were ruthlessly crushed. There was really nothing in the way of collective effort or any consistent policy of action. The magnificent epic of the Spain of Charles V was a brilliant conjunction of individuals, and should be looked upon as such.

In the first half of the sixteenth century—the age of Charles V—the art of this élite of rulers, soldiers, ecclesiastics and administrators reflects the individualistic and international character of the history of their times. There was no unity or discipline, but an intoxicating discovery of the joy of living, of the possession of power and wealth.

This new power swept away everything that had made up the social collectivities of the Middle Ages. The old Spain, with its Christian, Jewish and Moslem communities living side by side, its craftsmen's guilds, its traditionally organized agriculture, its little bourgeois liberties—all dedicated to productive, honest work well done—fell victim to the hankering after larger geographical and economic horizons and to the greed for power and quick wealth. And so the old system of workshops gave way before the fashionable cult of the Italian *dolce vita* or gracious living, and the purely local was replaced by the international taste for grandeur in the Renaissance style.

The discovery of great wealth by a traditionally austere and modest society led to an all-out desire to embellish and bejewel everything; even architecture was treated in the manner of the silversmith *(platero)*, so becoming Plateresque. There never seemed to be enough room for ornamentation; spaces were filled with a luxuriance which seemed to spring not so much from a desire for ostentation as from a sincere and real joy.

In Italy and Flanders, the two cultural worlds visited by the Spaniards in the time of Charles V, they encountered new ideas: in Italy, the concept of healthy sensuality, and in Flanders, spiritual contemplation. The cultured élite in Spain was infected by the joyousness of Italian poetry and Neo-Platonism. This was the climate which gave rise to the poetry of Boscán and Garcilaso de la Vega, with its hymn to human love and its sweet, beautiful vision of nature, filled with echoes of Theocritus, Virgil and Horace. The influence of the Low Countries upon the Spaniards was felt through the mystic meditations of Thomas à Kempis, but also in the lucid optimism of Erasmus.

4

THE DISCOVERY OF THE JOY OF LIVING

Nothing can give us a better idea of the character of the art of the age of Charles V than a look at the palaces built by the great leaders of the time. Long before the idea of Empire originated, and long before a powerful state had been consolidated, the war lords and the princes of the Church who traveled throughout Europe, already familiar with the delights of Arabic Andalusia, were won over to an Italian-style appreciation of the sweets of life, and they superimposed these new tastes upon the enchantments of the Nasrides of Granada.

The work done by the great Segovian architect Lorenzo Vázquez for the powerful family of the Italianate Cardinal Mendoza is a perfect illustration of the introduction of these new ideas. The Catholic Kings were still on the throne when Vázquez built an extremely Italianesque palace at Cogolludo in the province of Guadalajara for Luis de la Cerda y Mendoza. In this mansion he combined the new Italian techniques with some themes and even some decorative details of local origin widely used in the style of the Catholic Kings, mixed with northern Flamboyant motifs. Following the latest fashion from Florence, he devised a monumental harmonious façade of perfect symmetry—a symmetry which was to be observed in the interior arrangement. This façade has ashlar masonry, sturdily rusticated (reminiscent of the Medici, Pitti and Strozzi palaces in Florence), bipartite windows and a large classical cornice. The main portal, with its lunette crowned with palmettes, evokes, however ingenuously, the delightful creations of Michelozzo; the coat-of-arms is in the form of a laurel wreath, rather like a Brunelleschi *tondo*. But these Tuscan features are combined with Flemish-style pointed arches and the reliefs of dense arabesques which profusely decorate the windows and balustrade, whose Plateresque open-work is so finely wrought that it looks like Islamic damaskeening. On top is a ridge bristling with cresting, with regularly spaced pinnacles —a perfect example of Gothic ornament crowning a Renaissance structure.

This mixing of styles betokens a certain approach to life, the desire to confer upon the house of a powerful, wealthy person the dignified splendor of a palace, copying the serene grandeur of the palaces built by Florentine bankers and the refined, minute detail of the luxurious alcazars of the petty kings of Arabic Andalusia.

We find a similar fusion of styles in many buildings erected in this time of transition, a time when private wealth no longer looked to traditional ecclesiastical art as its model but began to turn to the highly pagan sources of inspiration of the Tuscan capitalists or the Moorish Nasride sovereigns, borrowing, too, some touches of Flemish richness. The high prelates of the Church were themselves seduced by the same siren songs when they designed their secular buildings with similar grandeur and luxury.

LORENZO VÁZQUEZ. PALACE OF THE DUKES OF MEDINACELI AT COGOLLUDO (GUADALAJARA). LATE 15TH CENTURY.

The Palace of Cogolludo was built for the first Duke of Medinaceli, a powerful nobleman who was related to the even more powerful cardinal of Santa Cruz, Pedro González de Mendoza, archbishop of Toledo.

Although there is no documentary proof, the design of this mansion can safely be ascribed to Lorenzo Vázquez, who started it soon after finishing the Colegio de Santa Cruz in Valladolid. When he took up this project, which was in fact sponsored by the cardinal of Santa Cruz, Lorenzo Vázquez had come into contact with the Italian style, not only through the cardinal's links with the Eternal City, but also and especially through the influence of that prelate's nephew, Diego López de Mendoza, Count of Tendilla, who was ambassador in Rome of the Catholic Kings.

Vázquez was engaged in the construction of the Colegio de Santa Cruz between 1489 and 1491, and immediately afterwards started on the Cogolludo palace, on which he worked, according to Gómez Moreno, from 1492 to 1495. In this structure he was able to develop those features of the Renaissance style which he had first tried out in Valladolid. Later, in the Castle of Calahorra in the province of Granada, he was able to develop this style even further, especially in the completely Florentine character of its courtyard.

AMPHITHEATER OF THE UNIVERSITY OF ALCALÁ DE HENARES. 1518-1519.

This hybrid style, sometimes called the "Cisneros" style, was introduced in such characteristic structures as the University of Alcalá de Henares and the Chapter Room of Toledo Cathedral. The earliest parts of the University of Alcalá, built on the orders of Cardinal Cisneros prior to the reign of Charles V, already show evidence of this style, but it reached its greatest heights under the Emperor. The amphitheater *(paraninfo)* has a paneled wooden ceiling, of richly carved tracery, designed by artists steeped in the Moorish tradition, bordered by Italian-style stuccos executed by Pedro Villareal, Bartolomé de Aguilar and Hernando de Sahagún in 1518 and 1519.

Perhaps even more characteristic are the Chapter Room and its vestibule of the Cathedral of Toledo. These magnificent rooms, designed by Pedro Gumiel, Cardinal Cisneros' architect, and Enrique de Egas, have carved wooden ceilings begun by Diego López and continued by Francisco de Lara. The painting is by Alonso Sánchez and Luis de Medina, who borrowed Florentine Renaissance themes—mouldings, torches, acanthus scrolls shaded in grisaille—and superimposed them upon the Moorish geometrical tracery.

The decoration of the vestibule is particularly lavish: the wood-paneling of the ceiling is bordered by Moorish-style plasterwork, Renaissance laurel wreaths, panels carved with classical acanthus leaves and mural paintings with foliage, garlands and architectural *trompe-l'œil*, the work of Diego López and the artists who were responsible for the decoration of the ceiling.

While these palatial interiors most vividly reflect the ruling society which, in the beginning of the sixteenth century, came into close contact with the rest of Europe, the American side of the Spanish adventure rarely finds expression in the plastic arts. However, we do have one memento of the age of the Conquerors in the monumental representation of the *Virgen del Buen Aire*, the "Virgin of the Good Wind," patron saint of navigators, painted by Alejo Fernández.

The vestibule of the Chapter Room of Toledo Cathedral was erected by Enrique de Egas and Pedro Gumiel between 1504 and 1512. Enrique de Egas was the architect in charge of the construction of the cathedral, while Pedro Gumiel was directly responsible to the cardinal archbishop. Naturally, there is every reason to believe that the architect of the cathedral would intervene in all technical matters, while the cardinal's architect would be responsible for seeing that the personal wishes of his master were faithfully interpreted.
The more purely decorative features were entrusted to Juan de Borgoña, assisted by Gregorio Pardo, Bonifacio Blondino and Gumiel himself, who did some of the carvings. The wooden paneled ceiling was begun by Diego López and continued after his death by Francisco de Lara, who completed it in 1508. In design this ceiling faithfully follows the patterns of Mudejar tracery, with its central motif of an eight-pointed star from which the interlacings spread out. The Mudejar stucco work of the walls is by Blondino, and the decoration, including grotesques, is by Gregorio Bigarny.

VESTIBULE OF THE CHAPTER ROOM OF TOLEDO CATHEDRAL.
BETWEEN 1504 AND 1512.

ALEJO FERNÁNDEZ (?-1543). THE VIRGIN OF THE NAVIGATORS. ALCÁZAR, SEVILLE.

Of German origin, Alejo Fernández studied in Italy and was greatly influenced by Flemish painting. In this picture he followed the general schema of the many portrayals of the Virgin of Mercy which appeared during the latter part of the Middle Ages: the large central figure is sheltering beneath her cloak those who have come to her for protection, suspended in the clouds above a sea dotted with ships. The line is supple, the colors are cold and silvery, and the Flemish technique of oil painting is used with great fluidity. This famous picture was painted for the chapel of the Seville Casa de Contratación, at that time the real seat of government of the Americas.

The conquerors who are sheltering beneath the cloak of the *Virgen del Buen Aire* (from whom the future capital of Argentina took its name) gave the example of the enjoyment of the good things of the material world to their fellow-countrymen at home. To provide a pleasant setting for their life, they conceived an art in which ornamentation and decoration were often the only qualities, since the pleasure they represent was not profound enough to change the basic principles.

CASTILIAN PLATERESQUE

During the age of Charles V architecture did not develop along the same lines in all his territories. In the eastern kingdoms inherited from the Catalonian Crown (Aragon, Catalonia, Valencia and Majorca), sparsely populated, center of a long-established, industrious but fragile Mediterranean empire, the need for conservation is reflected in the paucity of their artistic creativity or, at all events, in the pure Italianism of the forms used.

It was in the much more heavily populated dominions of the Crown of Castile, suddenly thrust into the stupendous American venture, that practically all the dynamic spirit and drive of the times were concentrated, and so it is there that the most characteristic works of this historic period are to be found.

Renaissance architecture in Castile falls into four distinct geographical regions. The first important area—the triangle formed by the basin of the River Duero—may be described as the Plateresque zone because of its fidelity to the spirit of the times of Mendoza and Cisneros, with their hedonism and love of rich decoration. It was the real heart of the Castilian states; of its three leading artistic centers—Salamanca, León and Burgos—Salamanca, the old intellectual and university capital of the country, was the most important.

The second of these regions is New Castile, or the basin of the Tagus; here new intellectual circles had been formed around the University of Alcalá de Henares and the ecclesiastical capital of the country, Toledo. Just as New Castile was the heir to Old Castile, and the University of Alcalá to the University of Salamanca, so the architecture of this region owed much to the Plateresque, although it showed fewer archaisms and was much more modern in spirit.

The third area is that of Granada, which had been a Moorish kingdom until 1492. Charles V wished to celebrate openly and ostensibly its union with Europe; he strove to foster a cosmopolitan spirit and violently suppressed all purely local rights and privileges. Very often in the history of art we see this phenomenon: countries steeped in tradition hold back when confronted by modern innovations and broader horizons, while those countries which break with tradition and accept new ideas in a new world understand, assimilate and experience intensely all that this newer and fuller world has to offer.

The fourth region of Renaissance art in the lands of Castile is that of Seville, the fabulous city that was the hub of all the vitality unleashed by the conquest of the Americas, the real political and economic capital of the Indies, through which all the riches of the New World had to pass, however briefly.

A great Andalusian capital like Granada, Seville had been invaded and taken over by the Castilians two centuries earlier. This dual national character is reflected in its art, which is a combination of the Plateresque style, more rooted in the traditional, and the newer classical style which found favor in Granada.

Salamanca owed its exalted position to the prestige of its University, the oldest in the Peninsula. A description of the capital of the Plateresque should, therefore, begin with this building, the very heart of the city. The façade of the University of Salamanca, designed by an unknown architect but attributed variously to Enrique de Egas, Pedro Manso and Juan de Torres, seems to have been erected between 1519 and 1525. Architectonically, it owes nothing to the Italian Renaissance; its origin must be sought in Andalusian Moorish architecture, as, for instance, in the portals of the Cuarto de Comares in the courtyard of the chapel of the Alhambra. The façade resembles a huge, well-proportioned rectangular tapestry where the profuse, detailed arabesques, almost uniform, evince a systematic abhorrence of a vacuum and are in striking contrast to the bareness of the adjacent walls.

This pattern was followed in such Mozarabic façades as that of the Alcázar of Seville, erected for the Castilian kings in the fourteenth century by architects inspired by the style of the Nasride dynasty of Granada. This concept was faithfully translated into Flamboyant decorativeness, romantic and exuberant, in the Late Gothic fronts

FAÇADE OF THE UNIVERSITY OF SALAMANCA, DETAIL. BETWEEN 1519 AND 1525.

built by Simón de Colonia for the church of Santa María la Real at Aranda de Duero (Burgos) and for the monastery of San Pablo in Valladolid. It was also to be imitated by one of his disciples in the remarkable façade which, with its profusion of plant forms mingled with exotic figures, crowns the doorway of the Colegio de San Gregorio, also in Valladolid, executed in the Late Gothic style known as Isabelline, direct forerunner of the Plateresque and the Portuguese Manueline style.

These successive changes in style were not really changes in concept. Moorish Nasride art and Mudejar, Flamboyant Gothic as well as Isabelline, were constant manifestations of the art of tapestry learnt from the Arabs and diametrically opposed to the classical. It was by definition an art of flat patterning, an art of matter rather than space, visual and not tactile, independent of its context and movable like a piece of furniture, and not fixed firmly in its surroundings; all idea of the concrete becomes lost in a tumult of forms and the mazes of an endless arabesque where there is no strong central accent.

Another influence to be seen in the façade of the University of Salamanca is that of Renaissance Grotesque, which was more typical of Lombardy than of Florence. A kind of tapestry of bas-reliefs crowns a Flamboyant structure of two segmental arches.

The façade is set out in rectangles, like those forming the panels above Moorish doorways; each rectangle, as well as the pilasters and friezes, is profusely adorned with acanthus leaf, armorial bearings, laurel wreaths and busts. These themes and figures express the meaning of the façade, like the Cufic inscriptions in Granada. In the lowest zone are the figures of the Catholic Kings who inspired the work. In the central part the escutcheon of Charles V is surrounded by the collar of alternate fire-steels and flints of the Flemish order of the Golden Fleece, between the Eagle of St John, protector of the Catholic Kings, and the double-headed imperial eagle of the House of Austria. In the center of the highest zone is the papal throne, surmounted by the tiara, symbol of the Church's teaching. It is crowned by the same kind of cresting as is found in the Medinaceli Palace at Cogolludo.

Old Salamanca is very rich in buildings of a similar nature, with some features of the Flamboyant style of decoration and luxuriant with Plateresque ornamentation: the church of San Esteban, designed by Juan de Álava, with a façade even more over-loaded with decoration than the Carthusian Monastery of Pavia, and the Colegio de los Irlandeses (seminary for Irish priests) built by Alonso de Covarrubias, which is almost like a smaller replica of the University.

But it is in the secular architecture of palaces and mansions, rather than in ecclesias-tical buildings, that the spirit of the age is better expressed. The most representative of the monuments of Plateresque architecture is beyond doubt a nobleman's palace, the Palace of Monterrey, which was begun in 1539. It was designed for Don Alonso de Acevedo y Zúñiga, Count of Monterrey, by Rodrigo Gil de Hontañón and his collabora-tor Fray Martín de Santiago, and built by Pedro de Ibarra and Pedro and Miguel de Aguirre, who were also responsible for the sculptural decoration.

Only one of its lateral façades was completed, but from this we can gain an idea of the grandeur that the main façade would have possessed if the building had been finished. It shows, too, that in only a few years Plateresque had developed from an amusing diversion borrowing themes from all sides—from Italy, Flanders and Islam—into a coherent and national style with a strong personality of its own.

The logical arrangement of this façade is comparable to that of the great Florentine façades, yet quite different. It is built up in layers, from a strong, thick base, austere and unadorned, to a light, ornate skyline, with the accent on strength decreasing and the embellishments increasing in beauty as it rises.

The massing and decoration of the Palace of Monterrey remind us of a tree with its robust trunk and abundant foliage. The ornamental cresting follows the rhythmical pattern of those of Cogolludo and the University of Salamanca, and can be seen as a final manifestation of the Gothic taste for open work.

Rodrigo Gil de Hontañón designed other noblemen's palaces in Salamanca, including the one built for the Fonseca family known as the Casa de la Salina. In León, where he also worked, he built the huge mansion of the Guzmán family. But his masterpiece is the graceful façade of the University of Alcalá de Henares, erected between 1543 and 1583, a clear and striking example of the Plateresque style of New Castile.

Examples of the Plateresque more rooted in the traditional are the buildings erected in Burgos by Francisco de Colonia, member of the German family "from Cologne" which worked in the cathedral, and by Diego de Siloe, son of the sculptor Gil de Siloe, also of German origin, who worked for the Catholic Kings. These include the Palaces of Saldañuela and Miranda, the Casa de los Cubos and the Casa de Angulo.

JUAN DE ÁLAVA. FAÇADE OF THE CHURCH OF SAN ESTEBAN IN SALAMANCA. 1524-1610.

RODRIGO GIL DE HONTAÑÓN AND PEDRO DE LA COTERA. FAÇADE OF THE UNIVERSITY OF ALCALÁ DE HENARES. 1543-1583.

In León, the masterpiece of the Plateresque style is the façade of San Marcos, impressive both in its monumental size and in the richness of its decoration. It was erected between 1533 and 1541 by Juan de Horozco, on plans drawn up by Pedro de Larrea. The arrangement is extremely rhythmical: groupings of two elements alternate with single elements. The decoration is as profuse as that of the Carthusian Monastery of Pavia and recalls other, non-Italian, Renaissance fronts—the ones in the courtyard of the Louvre, of the Palace of Heidelberg, for example. Semicircular embrasures and flat arches, paraments and niched shells, garlands and medallions, cornices and cresting —all are combined in a spirit of free fantasy.

The imposing Alcázar of Toledo is a unique example of New Castilian Renaissance architecture, and evokes better than any other monument the time when the city was virtually the capital of Charles V's empire. This massive pile, with its four sturdy towers, standing on the highest ground in Toledo, dominates and dwarfs the whole city. It was the product of several different epochs, but its chief architect—the one who was most responsible for its monumental grandeur—was Alonso de Covarrubias, working on the orders of the Emperor himself. Covarrubias studied both architecture and sculpture in the school of the Colonia family in Burgos. He went through a Gothic period before turning to Plateresque, and finally gave to this style the purity and serenity which typify the second, more refined phase known as purist Plateresque. In this purist style, the rhythm is slower, there are more empty spaces, decoration is more refined and more concentrated, proportions are vaster and nobler, and the whole becomes much more important than the details in this limpid, monumental architecture which is no less elegant for all its grandiosity. All the archaic features derived from Gothic, Flemish and Moorish art characteristic of early Plateresque have disappeared.

The façade of the Alcázar of Toledo, begun by Alonso de Covarrubias in 1538, is the most typical expression of this purist Plateresque style. It recalls in many ways the Palace of Monterrey in Salamanca; but the arrangement is quite different in that the lower part is less severe and more elegant while the upper part is more harmonious and restrained, with none of the decorative foliation found on the Salamanca building.

With the Hospital de Tavera, also in Toledo, begun in 1541 according to the original design of Bustamante, Covarrubias' style has become even more simplified, and purer. With its Italianesque courtyards surrounded by spacious arcades, this structure has a grandeur that is joined to the most refined elegance.

The Palace of the Archbishops at Alcalá de Henares is also the work of Covarrubias. His influence may have been a factor in the change that can be noted in the style of Rodrigo Gil de Hontañón from 1543 on, when he constructed a stone façade for the University of Alcalá de Henares, built in brick under Cardinal Cisneros. All the attributes of purist Plateresque that were indicated in the description of the Alcázar of Toledo can be found here, perhaps in even more refined form. The stress on smooth elegance is more pronounced here than in the Toledo building; the ponderousness as well as the rich foliation found in the Palace of Monterrey have completely disappeared. Soft curves predominate: in the archivolts of the segmental arch of the main doorway, in the Roman pediments and in the arcading of the upper storey.

The imperial coat-of-arms on the double-headed eagle of the House of Austria has pride of place in this simple but lively façade, which retains a last trace of the old open-work crestings of Germanic or Nasride origin, but in the form of a garland borne by *putti* in the style of the Rossellino brothers or Desiderio da Settignano.

GRANADA: THE UNIVERSAL SPIRIT

Unlike the Castilian schools of architecture, the school of Granada cannot be described as Plateresque. Here the Renaissance triumphed and flourished in its most universal form, most faithful to the canons of the ancient Roman, ecumenical tradition and to the precepts of contemporary Italian teachers.

Charles V decided to build an imperial palace on the wonderful hill of the Alhambra, in the very heart of the last fortress of Islam in Europe. This palace would express in the loftiest and purest way the image of the Europe which had just conquered that bastion. The design of this royal residence was therefore put in the hands of Pedro Machuca, who was able to execute it in a spirit that was completely European in its search for classical norms and universalist concepts.

Both architect and painter, Pedro Machuca had studied in Florence, perhaps working in the atelier of Giuliano da Sangallo, at the beginning of the century. As a painter, he is thought to have been a direct follower of Raphael. We know that in 1524 he was already working as a painter in Granada, where Charles V commissioned him to build his palace.

Construction was started around 1527 and supervised by Pedro Machuca until 1550, when his son Luis took over. After the death of Luis the work was carried on by Juan de Orea under the direction of Juan de Herrera and, later, Juan de Mijares. Building operations ceased in 1633, for lack of funds, and the palace has never been completed.

It is built in the form of a quadrangle, around a circular courtyard; in a typically classical manner it was planned with absolutely no regard to the surrounding country-side or the nearby Nasride palace. The arrangement of the interior is determined by the regular proportions of the exterior; it is divided into areas, all of which are rectangular except for a gallery and the octagonal chapel, placed in an angle.

The façades are two storeys in height, each of which has two levels of openings, following the Italian arrangement of mezzanines or half-storeys. The ordonnance is harmonious and methodical: the lower part is rusticated, the upper part smooth. The classical orders are superimposed according to established norms, Tuscan below and Ionic above. The embrasures are surmounted by acroteria alternating with pediments, and there are massive middle sections, in high relief, with matching double engaged columns. But the most original feature of this palace is the magnificent circular courtyard, which is surrounded by two superimposed linteled colonnades, also Tuscan in the lower stage and Ionic in the upper.

Quintessence of classicism, the Palace of Charles V is the purest example of the style of architecture developed in Granada during the sixteenth century, but it is not the only one. Several Italians were also working there, including Francesco Florentino and his brother Jacopo Florentino; the latter, also called Jacopo L'Indaco, had worked with Michelangelo in Rome. It was these two Florentines who built the Palace of the Vélez in Vélez Blanco, the church of San Jerónimo in Granada and the tower of Murcia Cathedral. All these works are characterized by the grandeur of the overall design combined with an almost precious fastidiousness in the decorative details which adorn them, albeit sparingly.

The architectural style initiated in Granada by Pedro Machuca and the Florentino brothers was brilliantly continued by Diego de Siloe, member of one of those German families of sculptor-architects settled in Burgos of whom we have already spoken.

Although he had received his early training in the Plateresque school, Diego de Siloe had studied in Italy together with his fellow-citizen, the sculptor Bartolomé Ordóñez. When, in 1528, he was assigned to take over the building of the church of San Jerónimo in Granada, begun by Francesco and Jacopo Florentino, he was able to set aside minor projects and to carry out his ambition to produce something vast, spacious and simple in the purest classical style. This first essay in the Granada style was followed by his greatest achievements: the Cathedral of Granada and, it is believed, the Cathedral of Malaga. These buildings are remarkable for their spaciousness, gentle rhythm, sober restraint, luminosity and purity.

Tiziano Vecelli—Titian—was Charles V's favorite painter. If Titian had been available, the Emperor would have liked to monopolize his talents to add lustre to his reign. Charles commissioned a number of pictures from the Venetian master, including several portraits of himself. Two of these are to be found in the Prado Museum. The first is *Charles V with a Dog*, a full-length portrait in which the Emperor is shown in the costume he wore when he was crowned King of Lombardy, accompanied by his dog—possibly the one called Sampere. This portrait was painted in Bologna between 1532 and 1533, and earned for Titian the title of Count of the Lateran Palace and Court Counsellor.

The other portrait in the Prado Museum, the *Emperor at the Battle of Mühlberg*, is the more important of the two. Charles V is mounted on his Spanish horse on the day of the Battle of Mühlberg, clad in full armor—the actual armor which can be seen today in the Royal Armory in Madrid—and grasping his lance. The river Elbe flows in the background.

The painting celebrates the victory of the imperial armies over the Protestants on April 24, 1547, the battle in which John Frederick of Saxony was wounded and taken prisoner.

Titian painted it in Augsburg between the months of April and September, 1548. He had left it out to dry in the open air when a gust of wind blew it against a post. The section showing the horse's croup was damaged and had to be repainted—by Titian himself. The picture was sent to Spain with Maria of Hungary and was placed in the Casa del Tesoro and in the Pardo Palace. It was in the Alcázar of Madrid when this building was destroyed by fire in 1734, and suffered some very slight damage of no importance.

TITIAN (1477-1576). EQUESTRIAN PORTRAIT OF THE EMPEROR CHARLES V AT THE BATTLE OF MÜHLBERG. 1548.
PRADO, MADRID.

PEDRO AND LUIS MACHUCA.
EXTERIOR OF THE PALACE OF CHARLES V IN THE ALHAMBRA OF GRANADA. 1527-1633.

It is interesting to note that Granada Cathedral, like the Palace of Charles V in the Alhambra, had a symbolic significance in that it represented the triumph of the European spirit in the last capital on the continent to be wrested from Islam. That is why Charles V personally defended the universalist conceptions of the Renaissance as represented by the art of Diego de Siloe against popular taste in Granada which would have preferred to keep to the Late Gothic style of the plans originally drawn up in 1521 by Enrique de Egas.

The most important part of Granada Cathedral, the chancel, was completed in 1540. It is a rotunda with a domed roof 72 feet in diameter and 148 feet high, ringed by an ambulatory, with two superimposed sets of Corinthian columns backed by pilasters, with two storeys to each order. This rotunda looks rather like an awkward addition to the nave, which had to be continued on earlier foundations.

The magnificent, spacious Cathedral of Malaga shows much more unity of style; following the idea that Rossellino developed in the Cathedral of Pienza, in Tuscany, four engaged columns support a graceful vaulted ceiling of cupolas upon pendentives. The general design was Diego de Siloe's, but it was given final form and constructed by Diego de Vergara and Andrés de Vandaelvira.

Andrés de Vandaelvira, who worked in Úbeda, Baeza, Jaén and Granada, was a more faithful follower of Italian models. The plan he drew up in 1532 for the Cathedral of Jaén is very similar in style to that of Malaga. Although his palaces, such as the one built for the Counts of Guadiana in Úbeda, are still Plateresque in spirit, some of his works are in the purest Roman style, like the sacristy of Jaén Cathedral, which is lined with full Corinthian columns set in pairs in two storeys; while others, such as the sacristy of the Salvador church in Úbeda, may be compared with the Florentine chapels of Bernardo Rossellino.

PEDRO AND LUIS MACHUCA. CIRCULAR COURTYARD OF THE PALACE OF CHARLES V IN THE ALHAMBRA OF GRANADA. 1557-1568.

DIEGO DE SILOE AND DIEGO DE VERGARA. INTERIOR OF MALAGA CATHEDRAL. BEGUN IN 1528.

We find the same kind of duality in the architecture of Seville. Diego de Riaño, who in collaboration with Martín Gainza erected the Plateresque palace of the Ayuntamiento (City Hall) and the equally Plateresque main sacristy of the Cathedral, achieved a Roman majesty in the chapter room of this same cathedral. Designed in 1530, it is oval in shape, sober and restrained; the Ionic order predominates.

The career of Diego de Riaño is an interesting and significant one. Although he himself was not Andalusian, he played a key part in shaping the character of Renaissance architecture in Seville. He was born in the north, possibly not far from Santander, and lived for a time in Valladolid. There he began the new cathedral, which was pulled down to make way for a construction planned by Herrera. His background was the school of Old Castile; and so his work was rooted in the typically Plateresque style which prevailed in that region. When he moved to Andalusia, however, he was brought into contact with the more classical, grandiose spirit radiating from the new Granada style.

Most of his time in Seville was spent on the Casas Capitulares, now the City Hall; he was in charge of building operations from 1527 to 1534, the year of his death in Valladolid. The major part of the actual construction was, in fact, carried out after his death, but keeping to his unmistakably Plateresque design. The façade was completed in 1564, and the interior decoration in 1573. Grotesques, medallions, bouquets and garlands, centaurs and sirens, real or imaginary animals, and a multitude of delightful *putti* adorn all the architectural surfaces. French, Flemish and Italian sculptors collaborated with Spanish artificers to produce this impressive display.

The basic concept of this construction seems to be completely at variance with that of the above-mentioned sacristy of Seville Cathedral, which is attributed to the same architect, Diego de Riaño. It is known that he received the commission in 1529, that the plans were ready by 1530, and that the actual building got under way in 1532. It is believed that Pedro Machuca was asked to design Charles V's Palace in Granada in 1526 and that the plans were already drawn up and approved in 1527. This means that when Diego de Riaño designed the City Hall in Seville he may not yet have known what Pedro Machuca was producing in the new serene, monumental style in Granada; his horizons were still limited to the preciosities of the Castilian style. When he undertook the sacristy for Seville Cathedral, however, there is no doubt that he was fully aware of what the Granada palace would be like. This explains why the dominant mood of the design for this sacristy is one of grandeur; it also explains his predilection for columns, the grand simplicity of its proportions and the classical feeling for space. De Riaño's Castilian heritage, on the other hand, explains the profusion of decoration, the almost Baroque use of twisted column shafts, the capitals adorned with animal figures, the plentiful anthropomorphic grotesques, the dragons, lions, garlands and fleurons. The mixing of styles which became characteristic of Renaissance architecture in Seville, when that city was the capital of the Americas, has its roots in this work.

THE EUROPEAN SPIRIT

The exaltation of man, the very essence of the ideas borrowed from the Italian Renaissance, was transformed by the Emperor into the exaltation of his own glory and sway. When we say, therefore, that the art of the age of Charles V was that of a few powerful figures each pursuing his own interests and concerns, we should not fail to include amongst these figures the Emperor himself; the marvels of the plastic arts were needed to bolster and serve his own exalted position.

The use of art for political ends was to become widespread, but Charles V was one of the first exponents of this practice. The fact that he embodied the basic ideas of Caesarism to an extent unknown in the immediate past, enabled Charles V to enter into an agreement with his artists similar to that which had existed between kings and jurists since the beginnings of Humanism.

For some time, especially since the thirteenth century, European monarchs had found the ideas of Roman law to be a most effective instrument in building up their power over the feudal lords. In this way men of law were enabled to rise to the highest ranks of society and a *noblesse de robe* came into being comparable to the hereditary nobility of military origin.

This agreement with the jurists was in the nature of a new feudal pact, in that the jurists provided a solid base for the King's authority and received in return the favors of power, money and social position. In the new Renaissance type of Caesarism of Charles V, artists were called upon to provide another, effective support for the royal power—by giving this power a physical shape, making it visible and tangible. In exchange, an era for artists would open up in which their names would become known and held in high esteem as those of the artisans of earlier times had never been.

Not only did the architecture of the time proclaim the King's pre-eminence, as in the incomparable, imposing proportions of the Alcázar of Toledo and the peerless Roman purity of the Palace of the Alhambra; the figurative arts and the crafts, too, made their contribution to the projecting of this radiant image.

The military ventures through which the Emperor and his followers sought to achieve their idea of glory have been portrayed for us in a rather special way in the tapestries with which they adorned their palaces. It was at this time that the art of tapestry-weaving reached its apogee in Brussels, which succeeded Tournai as the leading center in Europe. The materials used in the Brussels tapestries reached the highest standard of perfection; gold and silver threads were mixed with dyed wool to add lustre and

THE CONQUEST OF TUNIS BY CHARLES V. TAPESTRY FROM THE "CONQUEST OF TUNIS" SERIES DESIGNED BY JAN VERMEYEN. ESCORIAL.

refinement to the colorings. Scenes of battle were unfolded in huge panoramas; very high vanishing lines made it possible to appreciate at the same time the figures in the foreground and the vast scenes of armies, battles or besieged cities spread out in the background. Framing all this were decorative borders of foliage, with a profusion of flowers and fruit—all the subjects of still life—carefully executed in minute detail. Perhaps the finest examples of this period were produced in the ateliers of Willem Pannemaker, under the patronage of Charles V.

The Spanish Court, as well as the Church, greatly appreciated this type of work. The collection of tapestries in the Royal Palace in Madrid is the richest in the world, but those in the cathedrals of Tarragona, Saragossa, Burgos and Zamora are also worthy of attention; both their quantity and their quality reflect the international character of the plastic arts during the reign of Charles V.

BREASTPLATE OF THE ARCHDUKE ALBERT. ARMORY OF THE ROYAL PALACE, MADRID.

HELMET OF CHARLES V WITH RELIEFS REPRESENTING ROMAN KNIGHTS IN BATTLE. ARMORY OF THE ROYAL PALACE, MADRID.

Of all the series designed in Brussels for the glorification of Spanish might, the most monumental, and also the most historically significant, is the set depicting Charles V's conquest of Tunis, beginning with the departure of the expedition on the beach of Barcelona. The cartoons were made by Jan Vermeyen and the weaving was done in the workshops of Willem Pannemaker.

Another direct reminder of the military exploits of Charles V is the large collection of arms and armor—field and parade—housed in the Royal Armory in Madrid. Here again, there are many examples of "European" art which knew no frontiers; the best exhibits are from Augsburg where, under the influence of the Renaissance, a renowned, old-established metal-work industry had also turned to the representation of people and battles.

It was natural that a soldier-emperor should appreciate the use of metal as a means of plastic expression; that is why the bronze sculptures created by the Italian artist Leone Leoni in his honor seem to express the very spirit of his reign as very few other works of art do. Leoni, a native of Arezzo, also worked in marble, but his greatest achievements are his bronze figures of Charles V, the Empress Isabella and other members of the royal family.

The most interesting of these is without doubt the huge statue representing *Charles V defeating the Fury,* now in the center of one of the rotundas of the Prado Museum. An interesting point is that the statue of the Emperor is in reality a nude, like a hero of antiquity in the tradition of Verrocchio and Benvenuto Cellini, but provided with a detachable suit of armor.

In its feeling of movement, in the grouping of figures in space, in the profusion of accessories such as the lance and chains, it is a work which marks a breaking-away from former trends in sculpture depicting religious or royal subjects. It is not like an icon, designed to represent a single, sacred subject, but forms a complex free-standing group, which can be seen in the round from any angle—a group, furthermore, which is penetrated by air and light through its numerous internal spaces, following the Hellenistic model of the Farnese Bull, but showing great realism in its modeling and in its details.

A more sober and static style, which was to have a certain influence on the Spanish sculpture of his time, is to be seen in some of Leone Leoni's other portraits of royalty, for example the majestic figure of the Empress Isabella. In the works he created for the Church, we find the same combination of realism and majesty, and a desire to blend the work with its surroundings, especially in the bronze statues that he did for the main altar of the Escorial. These represent the twelve apostles, the Crucifixion (with an Apolline crucifix), a Virgin with the look of a Roman matron and a rather

LEONE LEONI (1509-1590) AND POMPEO LEONI (ABOUT 1533-1608). TOMB OF CHARLES V AND HIS FAMILY, DETAIL. 1593.
MAIN ALTAR OF THE CHURCH OF THE ESCORIAL.

asymmetric posture, in the manner of Michelangelo, and a St John with flowing drapery, heralding the Baroque in its overfullness and in the dark shadows of its modeling, yet still classical in its serenity.

The son of Leone Leoni, Pompeo Leoni, cast and completed the sculptures for the Escorial in his father's workshop in Milan and executed the funerary group of Charles V and his family. He became a specialist in funerary sculpture, a genre particularly suitable to the "black" mood of Spain towards the end of the sixteenth century.

An eloquent introduction to the black world of Philip II is provided by the bronze effigies of his family cast by Pompeo Leoni and set up in the Capilla Mayor of the church of the Escorial.

These impressive groups, representing Charles V and his family on one side of the main altar and Philip II and his family on the other, dramatically set in dim vaults, have nothing in common with the joyful spirit of the age of Charles V. They enshrine the love of the tragic which was so much a part of the times of Philip II and Philip III.

The two groups are made up of huge kneeling figures over twelve feet high, in bronze gilded and colored in predominantly dark shades. Charles V is decked out in his armor and an ermine cloak, and is shown with the Empress Isabella, his daughter Maria and his sisters, the Infantas Maria and Eleanor. Philip II is accompanied by three of his wives and his son, the Infante Don Carlos. Sombre, in a sombre setting, these ghostly figures are brightened only by the colors of their huge escutcheons, and portray for all posterity that world of "bewitched men" of whom the Memorial of Cellorigo speaks.

The evocation of death—this is the fundamental theme of the *Spiritual Exercises* of St Ignatius of Loyola, and it is a characteristic feature of Spanish art and indeed of the Spanish temperament.

Pompeo Leoni did not by any means stand alone in this field of funerary sculpture which captures the image of the whole age. Juan de Arfe copied the idea of the famous Escorial groups in his bronze sculptures for the tomb of Cristóbal de Rojas y Sandoval, Archbishop of Seville, in the collegiate church of San Pedro in Lerma, near Burgos. This is an impressively realistic work, begun by Juan de Arfe in 1602 and completed by Lesmes del Moral.

When he signed the contract for this sculpture Juan de Arfe undertook to execute it "with his own sinful hands, with no need of Italians"—an interesting and significant phrase which shows us that at that time and in Arfe's circle it was thought necessary to call upon someone from Italy for a work of high standard.

JUAN DE ARFE AND LESMES DEL MORAL. FUNERARY STATUE OF CRISTÓBAL DE ROJAS Y SANDOVAL. 1602-1603.
COLLEGIATE CHURCH OF SAN PEDRO, LERMA (BURGOS).

SALÓN DE CORTES (MEETING ROOM) IN THE PALACIO DE LA GENERALIDAD, VALENCIA. 1540-1566.

DECORATIVE ART

The age of Charles V saw the development of a style of decoration of the places and things which provided the setting for life—a style that looked more and more towards classical models and tended to turn away from the Flamboyant and Mudejar features which had been predominant in the early years of the century.

This tendency can be clearly seen when we compare works made of similar materials and intended for similar uses: for example, if we compare the paneled ceilings of the amphitheater of the University of Alcalá de Henares or the Chapter Rooms of Toledo Cathedral with other wooden ceilings like that of the Meeting Room (Salón de Cortes) of the Palacio de la Generalidad in Valencia, begun in 1540 by Ginés Linares and completed in 1566 by Gaspar Gregori.

What most characterizes this paneled ceiling in Valencia, designed on the purest Renaissance lines, is the gallery which runs around it. An order of composite columns resting upon pilasters is superimposed upon another, smaller one of arcades upon colonnettes in the form of candelabra, in the style of those in the Certosa of Pavia. All these, besides the balustrades and the corbels, are lavishly carved with figures, animals, palmettes, festoons and grotesques of every description.

During the sixteenth century weaving and embroidery received a fresh impetus; in finish and quality of materials used, a standard was reached far beyond anything that had been attained up to that time. Toledo was justly famed for its velvets; but the

Although manuscript illumination was essentially a medieval art, it continued to flourish in the scriptoria ▶ of cathedrals and monasteries, sometimes well into the eighteenth century. The development of printing became a practical reality; but, paralleling what happened with other processes of industrialization, while the old manual system of book production was condemned as being uneconomic, at the same time it was raised to the level of a luxury technique, the province of men or institutions who wished to provide themselves with *objets de luxe*. The powerful cardinals of Renaissance Toledo highly appreciated the art of illumination as being one of the mainstays of their glorious position. During the first third of the sixteenth century Cardinal Jiménez de Cisneros ordered the preparation of the famous *Rico Missal* in seven volumes. Its profuse decoration is a synthesis —typical of the period—of Flemish themes, French taste and the innovations of the Italian Renaissance. Much more in the Renaissance style is another product of the Toledo art of manuscript illumination, still displayed in the cathedral, a missal also done for a cardinal, Cardinal Tavera, patron of the arts. Its decorative themes, illustrating a variety of stories and vignettes, have a great deal in common with those which Italian and Spanish artists were using to adorn the walls of the Escorial, very much within the Mannerist fashion. Gómez Moreno sees a relationship between the style of the illustrations of this missal and that of Francisco de Comontes, whose work was also most decidedly Italianate. Actually, in spite of the Italianism of the forms and themes, there are still traces of Flemish-inspired realism, which finds expression in the minute and exact treatment of details such as flowers, fruit, birds, butterflies and other insects.

ILLUMINATED MISSAL OF CARDINAL TAVERA: CHRIST ON THE CROSS. 16TH CENTURY. CATHEDRAL LIBRARY, TOLEDO.

EMBROIDERED COPE OF THE 18TH CENTURY, WITH 16TH-CENTURY ESCUTCHEON. CATHEDRAL MUSEUM, TOLEDO.

cities recently taken from the Moors, like Valencia, Murcia and especially Granada, were also important weaving centers, specializing in plain or brocaded silks, frequently using gold and silver threads.

The fabrics woven in the age of Charles V, often resembling those of Damascus, had characteristic floral patterns, motifs of lobate leaves and huge pines, at first treated asymmetrically in the Venetian style and later on boldly symmetrical.

The vestments of the bishops of Toledo would have to be exceptionally luxurious, and so it has been possible to preserve in the Cathedral of Toledo a rich treasure-house of more than forty exhibits, especially chasubles, dalmatics and copes. The fame of the great embroiderers who decorated these vestments has also been handed down—master craftsmen like Maestre Jacques, Martín Ruiz, Marcos de Covarrubias, Juan de Talavera, Francisco de la Riva and Esteban Alfonso.

Other examples of luxuriously fashioned religious articles were choir books, missals and prayer books. In them the medieval art of miniature painting was continued, although translated into Renaissance terms. Great quantities of these books are to be found in the Cathedral of Toledo, the Monastery of Guadalupe, the Cathedral of Seville and the Royal Chapel of Granada.

THE REDISCOVERY OF THE HUMAN BODY

In the Castilian states Gothic sculpture had been first and foremost a visual sculpture, in which chiaroscuro values had been uppermost. This visualism came from a profound sense of the symbolism of light and darkness, related to spiritualism and implying a negation of the tangible as being corporal and inferior. This fundamentally anti-materialist negation led to an art form in which there were no strong accents, as though there were no such thing as personality but only the infinite wonder of a blurred, indistinct background.

With the Renaissance emerged a feeling for the tangible which inspired not only an appreciation of the concept of mass and the values of protruding light surfaces, but also of all those values of spatial organization which proceed not from visual experience, as do light and shade, but from tactile experience, like perspective and the precise use of space. The development of a sculpture of mass and spatial expression led to the birth of rhythm and movement. Plain or distant backgrounds made their appearance.

VASCO DE LA ZARZA. TOMB OF "EL TOSTADO." 1520-1524. AMBULATORY OF AVILA CATHEDRAL.

With the assistance of the master craftsman Ficate and later the foreign artisans Charles and Robert, Juan de Badajoz began work on the retrochoir of León Cathedral in 1529. The statues and panels were executed by Juan de Juní and Esteban Jordán at the end of the century. This ensemble furnishes one of the most extreme examples of the preciosity found in the sculpture of the Plateresque era. The exquisite, exaggeratedly slender columns, the robust consoles of the socle, the volutes of the crowning ornament, the surbased intrados, segmental arches, medallions crowded with figures—all help to give a heightened sense of movement and chiaroscuro. It has an agitation and a liveliness which may be due to the backgrounds of these artists, who were trained in the schools of Burgundy or Flanders.

This *trascoro*, or retrochoir, was begun during the bishopric of Don Pedro Manuel. Juan de Badajoz had begun the construction of León Cathedral when this bishop was appointed to the see, in 1523. Six years later he started work on the retrochoir. It was not without some difficulty that the cathedral chapter was persuaded to approve the plans, since many of the canons were opposed to Renaissance innovations which no doubt seemed to them to be expressions of paganism quite out of keeping with the character of a holy shrine. But Bishop Pedro Manuel's ideas prevailed, and Juan de Badajoz's design was carried out with the help of the master craftsmen and artisans mentioned above and of the sculptors Pedro de Salamanca and Guillén Doncel.

The *trascoro* is in the form of an oblong wall; in the center there is an open archway, 16 feet wide by 25 feet high, with niches on each side, on a high podium, the inside of which is covered with reliefs. When Bishop Pedro Manuel's period of office ended in 1534, the contribution of Juan de Badajoz came to an end, but the work was carried on by the sculptors Juan de Juní and Esteban Jordán. Upon Juní's death in 1577 it was continued by Jordán, who completed it in 1600.

ESTEBAN JORDÁN (1543-1603). RETROCHOIR OF LEÓN CATHEDRAL, DETAIL.

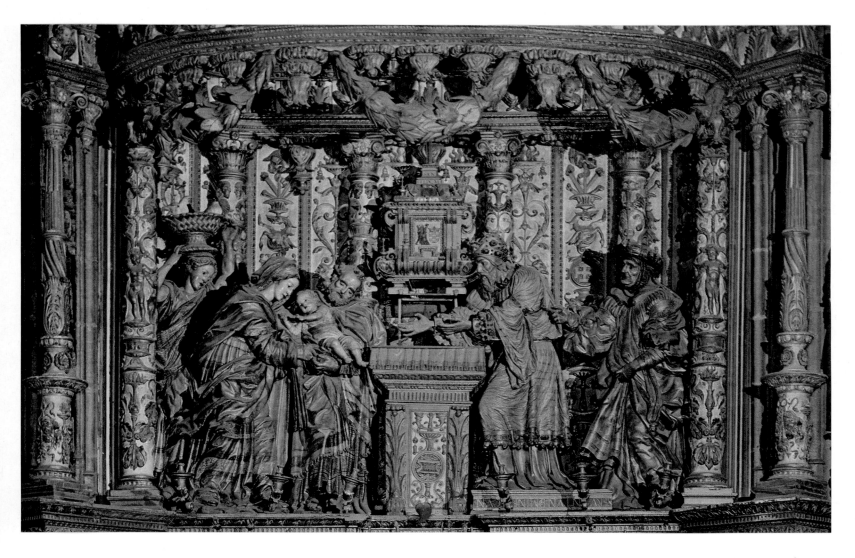

FELIPE BIGARNY AND DIEGO DE SILOE. RETABLE WITH THE PRESENTATION IN THE TEMPLE, DETAIL. 1523.
CHAPEL OF THE CONSTABLE, BURGOS CATHEDRAL.

The *horror vacui* gave way to a preference for empty spaces, pauses and harmonious compositions. The human body took on new meaning through gesture, and gesture was made to embody a sense of grandeur, nobility and majesty, very largely through the influence of a knowledge of the statuary of the Greeks and Romans often gained directly in Italy. The human figure was no longer lost in the general presentation —as had been the case hitherto when it was caught up in luxuriant foliage—but became the center of interest, worthy of being magnified.

It is interesting to note that while the Court accepted these concepts as reflecting their own view of life, the Church, in order to exercise its influence over the people, very often continued to favor the theatrical devices of visual qualities and did not relinquish the use of color and gilding, linearism and the interplay of bright projections and dark depressions, and even arabesque designs with their suggestion of the infinite.

DIEGO DE SILOE. ST JOHN THE BAPTIST, DETAIL OF THE THRONE OF THE BENEDICTINE ABBOT OF BURGOS. 1522-1528?
MUSEO NACIONAL DE ESCULTURA, VALLADOLID.

In this age of internationalism sculpture, like all the other art forms, was enriched by the influx of foreign artists, continuing a trend which had begun towards the end of the fifteenth century. One of the pioneers of the new sculpture was the Burgundian artist Felipe Bigarny, or Felipe de Borgoña, who arrived in Spain before the turn of the sixteenth century to work in the Cathedrals of Burgos and Toledo. He was converted to the Italian style through the influence of Jacopo Florentino. He was commissioned by Charles V himself to work in the Royal Chapel at Granada. His masterpiece is the retable of the Constable's Chapel in Burgos Cathedral, created in collaboration with the German sculptor Diego de Siloe.

The monumental composition of this altar and the important place given to gesture and the human body are Renaissance features; but Bigarny's Burgundian origins are revealed in a certain dramatic vibrancy, a tremulous arabesque and an emotivity which are seen not only in the agitated modeling, but also in the use of color and gilding. We find here many of what were to become the most characteristic features of Spanish religious sculpture.

The work of Vasco de la Zarza shows a similar compromise between a serene Renaissance style and an emotional Gothic one, between the restfulness of the tactile and the vibrancy of the visual. Just as Bigarny was converted to Italianism by Jacopo Florentino, Vasco de la Zarza—even before going to work in Italy—was influenced by Domenico de Alessandro Fancelli, an Italian sculptor who worked in Spain as a protégé of the Mendoza family. Zarza's most important work is the tomb of Alonso de Madrigal, known as El Tostado, which stands behind the altar in the chancel of Avila Cathedral, dating from 1520 to 1524.

This sculptured group, delicately carved in alabaster, is bland and genial, very Italianesque; the serene effigy of the bishop, portrayed as he was when alive and occupied at his daily task of writing, is as different from the rigid funerary effigies—with their mourners—of Gothic sculpture as it is from the exaggerations of Baroque. But sometimes, as in the *tondo* of the *Adoration of the Kings* behind this statue, a fondness for refined detail reflects the sculptor's Gothic background.

Diego de Siloe, the artist who collaborated with Bigarny in the retable of the Constable's Chapel and whose architectural activities have already been mentioned, had a greater impact; he was an artist of a more passionate stamp. From his studies in Italy, where he was in close association with Bartolomé Ordóñez, a follower of Michelangelo, Diego de Siloe acquired the almost superhuman, Michelangelo-like strength and vitality which flow through all his works. This is especially true of the wood carvings of the throne of the Benedictine Abbot of Burgos, which used to be in the choir of the monastery of Valladolid and is now in the National Sculpture Museum of that city.

ALONSO BERRUGUETE (1480/90-1561). FIGURE STUDIES. DRAWING. UFFIZI, FLORENCE.

The Uffizi Gallery contains several sketches by Alonso Berruguete that are of great interest. These sketches demonstrate the careful preparations, based on the study of anatomy, that this sculptor made before planning and executing his works. They show us the kind of poses he wanted to give to his figures, the exaggerated contortions which were intended to make them more highly expressive. The figures seen from behind turn their faces towards us, while those whose bodies are seen from the front turn their heads away from us; the ones facing right have their arms stretched out to the left; if they seem to be falling to the ground, their arms are reaching upwards. All this results in outlines that are sinuous and broken, asymmetric inner curves, and an interplay of light and shade that tends to give the figures rather the look of twisted column-shafts.

When this almost abstract concept is applied to themes of religious art, the counter-balance of the iconographic elements can soften the purely plastic effects. Thus the *Christ at the Column* has a certain Apolline bearing, but still shows something of the dislocated posture typical of Berruguete's twisted style: the head turned in the opposite direction to the feet, the outstretched arm contrasting with the leg held backwards, and the lowered shoulder with the raised hip.

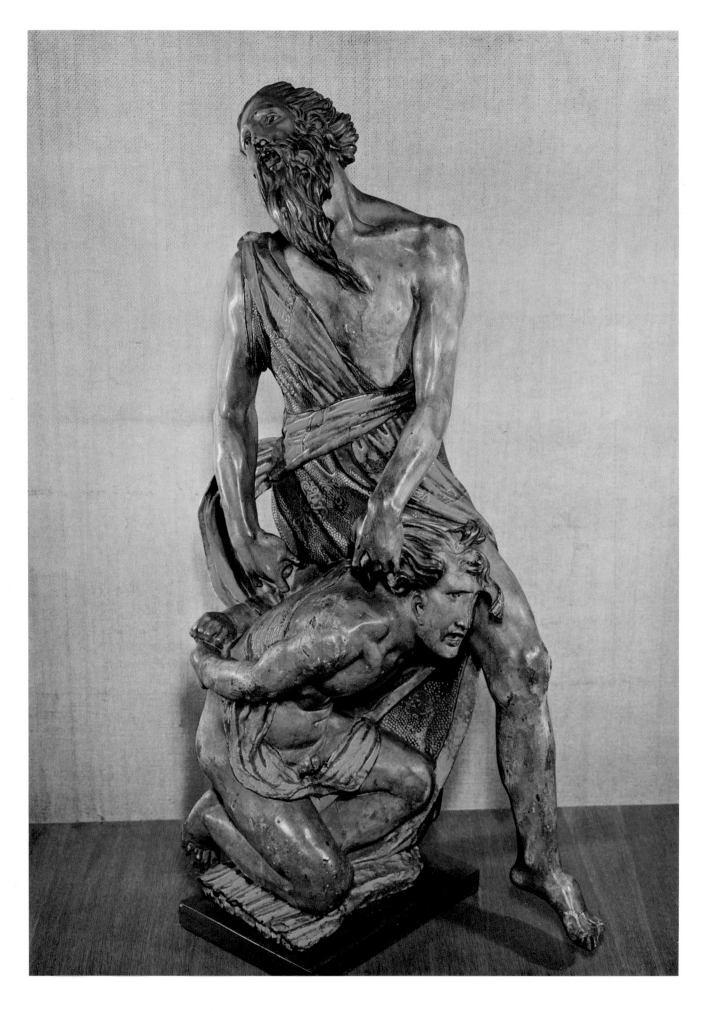

ALONSO BERRUGUETE (1480/90-1561). ABRAHAM AND ISAAC. 1527-1532. MUSEO NACIONAL DE ESCULTURA, VALLADOLID.

These reliefs, carved between 1522 and 1528—and particularly the most interesting of them, representing St John the Baptist—are a hymn of praise to the human body, through attitudes which are not merely aesthetic postures, as in ancient statuary, but an attempt to capture and embody the dynamic rhythms of an interior force, as Michelangelo did in the rendering of his figures. This relief carving of St John the Baptist by Diego de Siloe was the direct model for some of the most significant works of Alonso Berruguete, the most important Spanish sculptor of the sixteenth century.

Berruguete, a native of Palencia and son of the painter Pedro Berruguete who was one of the first Spanish artists to have been influenced by the Italian Renaissance in the fifteenth century, studied in Italy—for a time under Michelangelo himself. On his return to Spain he began to work as a painter rather than as a sculptor, though on the whole his paintings are uninspired; they seem rather to follow a formula than to spring from true conviction. His sculptures, on the other hand, show great individuality, and are executed with a conviction that often verged on fanfaronade. He was, indeed, very sure of himself and of his ideas, and had no qualms about maintaining that there was nobody in Spain who knew as much about sculpture as he did—which was undoubtedly true, so far as we can judge from the works that have come down to us.

Berruguete's art was passionate, strong and vigorous, sometimes bold, harsh and austere, but not without a sensitive touch at times, often defying the rules of anatomy and sometimes almost brutal. The sheer genius of his work compelled recognition, although it was not to the Emperor's taste—Charles V never gave official approval to his designs—nor, indeed, does it seem to have been to the general taste. He was the target of a great deal of criticism, but this did not prevent him from running his large collective atelier or from amassing a considerable fortune which enabled him to live in lordly fashion and build himself a palace in Valladolid; he acquired from the King the seigniory of Ventosa de la Cuesta, in Tierra de Campos.

His first important sculptured work was the high altar of the church of San Benito el Real, in Valladolid, commissioned when the artist was thirty-seven years old and actually begun when he was thirty-nine.

This retable is now preserved in the National Sculpture Museum in Valladolid. More than thirty figures, polychrome on a gilt ground, measuring between 31 and 43 inches in height, were carved for it. The most outstanding of these, and the ones which, in their tenseness, best represent Berruguete's creative power, are those of Abraham sacrificing Isaac, St Christopher, St Jerome and St Sebastian. The figure of Abraham is perhaps the tensest of all; it is an embodiment both of Abraham's impassioned surrender to God and of the agony of the decision he had to make, expressed in a muscular, hard style, contorted but not tortured. Remarkable in a similar way are a twisted St Christopher, an elongated St Sebastian and a vibrant St Jerome.

ALONSO BERRUGUETE (1480/90-1561). TWO PROPHETS. DRAWING. ACADEMY OF SAN FERNANDO, MADRID.

ALONSO BERRUGUETE (1480/90-1561). ST JOHN THE BAPTIST. CHOIR STALL IN TOLEDO CATHEDRAL. 1539-1548.

ALONSO BERRUGUETE (1480/90-1561). EVE. CHOIR STALL IN TOLEDO CATHEDRAL. 1539-1548.

In 1539 Berruguete was invited by the chapter of Toledo Cathedral to collaborate with Bigarny in the carvings of the cathedral choir stalls. Bigarny died four years later, and Berruguete was left to complete the great work alone: thirty-six reliefs in walnut for the back of the stalls and thirty-four in alabaster for the frieze above them, besides an alabaster group of the Transfiguration which crowns the choir.

In this series of figures he was able to give full rein to his power of evoking different psychological types and expressive attitudes. Some of the figures, like Mattathias, are seen from the back; some, like Methuselah, are shown from the front, bending forwards. Of the alabaster statuettes, Enoch is shown leaning slightly to one side, in the manner of the ephebes of classical sculpture. In walnut, undoubtedly the most inspired are the fiery figures, almost El Greco-like, of Jude Thaddaeus and John the Evangelist, the Verrocchio-style St Sebastian, the Michelangelesque St Catherine and the impassioned Noah and Moses.

There are two superb panels devoted to Eve and St John the Baptist. This Eve is the first completely nude female figure in Spanish art, and is rather reminiscent of the style of the reliefs of Jacopo della Quercia in San Petronio, Bologna, which Berruguete may well have seen during his stay in Italy. His St John the Baptist, no doubt inspired from Bigarny's carving for the choir of Valladolid, is a most expressive anatomical study, in which the hollows are as important as the projections and the asymmetrical modeling is as telling as the Scopas-like expression of the face.

ROMAN FANTASIES

The two great powers of the sixteenth century, the Crown and the Church, were both seeking to bring about a revival of the Roman Empire: the Crown because it was an Empire, the Church because it was Roman.

Both turned to the marvels of architecture as one of the means of bolstering up their authority. That is why the palaces of Charles V and the new cathedrals then being built in Andalusia—at Granada, Malaga and Jaén—were turned into impressive showpieces and organs of propaganda.

The Crown needed the prestige and glamour that architecture could give, hitherto the exclusive preserve of the Church; the Church needed as much spaciousness and the same high-flown style as had gone into the building of the Roman baths.

This dual cult of Roman architectonic ideas pervaded everything. The furniture of palaces and churches, tableware and monstrances, braziers and candelabra, were all affected by the prevailing fashion, this urge to adapt Roman architectural forms to all arts and crafts. The Renaissance was above all an architectural phenomenon, and even portable objects became a fantastic echo of the monumental.

The influence of this Roman cult radically affected that most characteristic Spanish object of worship, the *custodia*, or monstrance; this term is used to include the host itself, the stand on which it was exhibited and the shrine which held it.

This branch of the silversmith's art had been very flourishing in the Gothic era. The Arfe family had produced masterpieces of Flamboyant fancy, somewhere between the architectonic and the vegetal, imbued with a mysterious, almost hallucinatory power of suggestion, and comparable in this respect only with the Isenheim Altarpiece; the fabulous monstrance of Toledo Cathedral is an example of these elaborate, tower-like receptacles in which the host was displayed to the faithful.

The Renaissance took over this fantastic notion of considering the monstrance as a monument in miniature, and artists stubbornly maintained this concept even while translating it into the Romanized idiom.

It was this same Arfe family that provided the most important artificers of Renaissance monstrances in Spain. The first of them was Enrique, a German from a village near Cologne who had settled in Spain at the beginning of the sixteenth century. His works, highly esteemed during his lifetime, include the famous monstrance of Toledo Cathedral, commissioned by Cardinal Cisneros in 1515; it is based on the Flamboyant Gothic designs of artists trained in the Low Countries, such as Copín de Holanda and Juan de Borgoña.

But in the silver casket of San Froilán in León Cathedral, on which he started work in 1518, Enrique de Arfe used motifs from the thematic repertory of Italian Renaissance grotesques, although he handled them in a stiff, dry, uneven manner which reveals that he had some difficulty in adapting himself to the new style.

His son Antonio de Arfe, however, made full and graceful use of Italian Renaissance themes, both in the monstrance of the Cathedral of Santiago de Compostela, begun in 1539, and the later one for the church of Medina de Ríoseco, although he applied these themes to what was essentially a Gothic structure: a high podium with four superimposed prismatic aedicules, flanked by buttresses. All supports are in the form of slender balusters or candelabra, and a series of even smaller aedicules act as pinnacles. A great many figures in the round enliven this elaborate monstrance, which, crowded with grotesques, is a characteristic example of the fully developed Plateresque style.

PEDRO LAMAISON AND DAMIÁN FORMENT. MONSTRANCE OF SARAGOSSA CATHEDRAL. 1537-1541.

The metal-worker Antonio de Arfe was the son of Enrique de Arfe, a German silver-smith from the Cologne region married to a Castilian lady, Gertrudis Rodríguez Carreño; Enrique de Arfe was responsible for the famous Flamboyant-style monstrance in Toledo. Antonio de Arfe was born in León about 1510, and worked in his father's atelier, where his introduction of Renaissance forms was decisive. In 1539 he was commissioned by the chapter of the Cathedral of Santiago de Compostela to design the monstrance for this cathedral. The model, in wood, was ready in 1543, but the monstrance could not be executed immediately because of financial difficulties and differences of opinion between the artist and the chapter. Nevertheless, it was finally completed in 1545, six years after it was commissioned. While its architectural form represents a translation into Renaissance terms of an essentially Flamboyant conception, the sculptural features remind us of the tense, twisted style of Alonso Berruguete.

The family tradition was carried on by Juan de Arfe y Villafañe, a polished, cultured and erudite man, author of the treatise in prose and verse entitled *De varia conmensuración para la Escultura y Arquitectura*. His theories were completely Mannerist, and his aim was to purify architectural forms and make them colder, and to develop the typically Mannerist approach to the treatment of the column. In 1564 he began work on the monstrance for Avila Cathedral; between 1580 and 1587 he created the one for Seville Cathedral, based on allegorical themes devised by the scholar Francisco Pacheco. Very proud of his work, he asserted that it was "the greatest and best piece in silver of this kind that is known." Pedro Lamaison was commissioned to do the monstrance for the Church of Nuestra Señora del Pilar, Saragossa, in 1531. Because of the rivalry that existed between the main cathedral, *La Seo*, and the Pilar Church, he was asked to undertake another, much more important one, for the cathedral in 1537. The Valencian Damián Forment did the sculptural work from 1539 onwards.

The third of the Arfes, Juan de Arfe y Villafañe, "sculptor in gold and silver and architect," was the one who turned away from Plateresque and introduced Roman-style monumentalism. This highly skilled silversmith, sometimes referred to as the "Spanish Cellini," was a proponent of architectonic severity very much in keeping with the spirit of the age of Philip II, and expressed his theories in a didactic work, *De varia conmensuración para la Escultura y Arquitectura* (Seville, 1585), which sets forth very strict standards and rules.

It was Juan de Arfe y Villafañe who created the monstrances of Avila Cathedral (1564-1571) and Seville Cathedral (1580-1587). Over nine feet high, both were designed in architectonic terms as buildings in which the podiums, Ionic and Corinthian colonnades, arcading, aedicules, obelisks, Atlantes, pediments, balustrades, cupolas and sky-lanterns all reflect a desire for simplicity, a rejection of any embellishment not felt to be worthy of monumental architecture or sculpture.

The triumph of this Romanism meant that the day of many a Plateresque artist was over—craftsmen like Pedro Lamaison, whose processional monstrance for Saragossa Cathedral, started in 1537, is severe in its proportions but weighted down with ornament and crowded with a multitude of silver statuettes, the work of the Valencian sculptor Damián Forment.

Gold and silver were not the only metals considered to be worthy of special treatment by artists of the Spanish Renaissance. Iron, too, soon began to be treated with loving care from the time when the grating of the *reja*, or grille which formed the enclosure of a chapel or altar, was first twisted and embellished with forged and hammered work, initially only in medallions with busts, figures or laurel wreaths and, later on, in elaborate crestings, pilasters and friezes.

Francisco de Salamanca and Juan de Avila, both monks of the Monastery of Guadalupe, were amongst the first craftsmen of the sixteenth century to transform the making of grilles, a typically Spanish speciality, into a fine art in its own right.

Cristóbal de Andino was one of the first to introduce in these grilles a number of motifs borrowed from Renaissance architecture in the Roman manner. A famous architect, Francisco de Villalpando, who designed in 1541 the monumental grille which screens the high altar of Toledo Cathedral, was another exponent of this style.

Cristóbal de Andino, whose major work is the grille of the Constable's Chapel in Burgos Cathedral, used columns covered with grotesques, in the form of candelabra, and with curved base, and forms of urns, balusters and vases; on his friezes, with their griffins, busts and palmettes—and indeed on all the structural elements—he also used classical flower, fruit and leaf ornaments.

FRANCISCO DE VILLALPANDO. DETAIL OF THE ALTAR SCREEN OF TOLEDO CATHEDRAL. 1541-1548.

CABINET DECORATED WITH POLYCHROME MARQUETRY, FRONT. 16TH CENTURY.
MUNTADAS COLLECTION, MUSEO DE ARTES DECORATIVAS, BARCELONA.

Francisco de Villalpando's grille for the high altar of Toledo Cathedral is perhaps the
most grandiose in Spain. It is surmounted by a most agitated cresting: it has a cross
in the base of which slaves holding up candelabra—and bending over, like the slaves
of Michelangelo—are supported by the volutes that surround the enormous royal
escutcheon of the House of Austria, with its two-headed eagle and the collar of the
Order of the Golden Fleece; on each side are caryatids bearing baskets of fruit, beneath
graceful baldachins, grotesques with masks and hermae, not forgetting the two pillars
of Hercules inscribed with the ambitious royal device, PLUS ULTRA (which alludes
to the steady growth of the imperial power and its extension to all continents).

Another article which faithfully reflects the spirit of the age is the traditional piece
of furniture called in Spain the *bargueño*, an oblong cabinet made up of many small
drawers and compartments with doors, and often containing hidden nooks and
pigeon-holes; it had no legs and was placed on a table or any flat surface. This type
of cabinet, which had originally been a strictly utilitarian piece of furniture, was
gradually transformed into a monumental work of art in the Renaissance era. Cabinets
began to be embellished, on an increasingly lavish scale, with inlays of ivory, tortoise-
shell and polished wood (marquetry or intarsia), often with fanciful designs consisting
of incised lines filled in with a black substance, in a technique similar to that of niello-
work. The decorative motifs, sometimes including figures, were usually of conventional-
ized flora, in the Italian tradition; or else, much more in keeping with the contemporary
climate, they reflect the ideas behind some surrealistic architectonic creations, in unna-
tural perspective, conceived almost like the metaphysical paintings of Giorgio de Chirico.

CABINET DECORATED WITH POLYCHROME MARQUETRY, LEFT SIDE. 16TH CENTURY.
MUNTADAS COLLECTION, MUSEO DE ARTES DECORATIVAS, BARCELONA.

THE RIGORS OF THE COUNTER REFORMATION

The second half of the sixteenth century, which almost coincides with the reign of Philip II, was totally different from the age of Charles V, and in many aspects was the exact opposite. In territorial extent the Spanish Empire reached its maximum during this period. The new discoveries in America, Oceania and the Philippines, together with the annexation of Portugal and her dominions in America, Africa and Asia, made Philip II's Empire one of colossal dimensions.

But within Spain itself there were terrible weaknesses. A succession of costly wars had exhausted both the economy and the population, and bred discontent. The various states under the Crown were engaged in economic struggles amongst themselves: Castile, in alliance with Genoa, was trying to seize the Naples market from Catalonia and imposed a fifty per cent ad valorem customs duty on Catalonian textiles.

At the same time English privateers were ceaselessly active—these were the days of Drake and Hawkins—and took a heavy toll of Spanish merchant ships in the Atlantic, while the Turks and Algerines raided the Mediterranean coast of Spain, the royal fleet proving quite unable to prevent their depredations.

Many people had hoped that the gold and silver from Spanish colonies in the Americas would bring wealth to the country. But the treasure fleets were often intercepted by English privateers and the precious metals which reached Seville quickly found their way into the banks of the Continent, through Laredo and Antwerp, to pay off debts and finance the wars; and later, when wars and pirates had made the Atlantic dangerous, the riches passed from Barcelona to Genoa and thence to Besançon and Frankfort, to the fairs of Piacenza, to the war reserves kept in Milan, or else went directly to the Fugger family of German bankers to settle past debts.

The money that stayed in the Peninsula was not invested in production, but invested in State securities or in land. The loss of great numbers of men who went off to the Indies, or who entered the Church and the Army, resulted in a shortage of manpower, and those who stayed behind were not very productive. This meant that landowners were not able to amass capital. A shortage of food was caused by the exportation of wine, oil and flour—and corrupt viceroys and officials, who collected money from granting export licences, naturally encouraged these exports. This shortage led to a considerable rise in prices. As a result foreigners, whose prices were lower, took over trade inside Spain, even retail trade. First at the fair of Medina del Campo, then later setting up shops in Seville or Valencia, they effected a constant drain of money towards the continent.

INTERIOR OF THE CHURCH OF THE ESCORIAL. 1563-1584.

The only ones in Spain to benefit from the high prices were the Andalusian landowners, who turned to the single-crop production of wheat, oil or wine; the prices of these commodities doubled, tripled and went up eightfold respectively in the middle of the sixteenth century. This made it impossible for the small farmer to survive and so led to the creation of latifundia in Andalusia.

Speculation created a state of affairs in which, instead of men of action, there were soon only *rentiers*. This mentality also infected the State and put an enormous financial strain on the country. By the end of the sixteenth century—and of Philip II's reign— Spain was on the brink of economic ruin. The idea of great wealth and riches had been lost: there was only the idea of money in the abstract.

The disappearance of a productive spirit and the growth of a climate of speculation led to the situation described in the Memorial of Cellorigo, about 1600: "Nothing seems truer than that they wished to reduce these kingdoms to a republic of bewitched men who live outside the natural order of things."

With all this, in fifty years Spain had turned her back on the great European adventure of production and capitalism. The large commercial or banking fortunes amassed in Seville through the exploitation of the Americas were eaten up in luxuries and retinues of servants, or were invested without risk and so could not make any contribution towards continental development. If only for this reason Spain would have broken her links with Europe, even without the isolationist attitude of Philip II, who turned his back on the rest of Europe. He intervened in international problems only to play the ostentatious but illusory role of champion of Catholicism, which did not prevent him from following a policy of ruthless repression in the Netherlands.

The joyous age of Charles V was over: the Spanish Crown and Church joined forces in a zealous campaign to defend the Absolute—by the pen, by the sword, through the spoken word and through art. Spain *was* the Counter Reformation, and the Basque, Ignatius of Loyola, was its most powerful agent. Strict asceticism, solemn austerity, a proud solitude, a taste for black or pallid colors, and a lofty dignity set in, and made the Spanish Court into a model of stuffiness and stern etiquette.

From this time forward, and throughout the most complicated developments in Spanish thought, in a variety of changing social situations, certain traits can be seen to typify the Spanish character; once they were ascribed to the Court, henceforth they spread to those sectors of society where men's lives were still rooted in tradition and their concepts remained unchanged. Castilian asperity, pride, lordly bearing, contempt for a more passionate, dynamic way of life, lay at the root of the pallid world which was to be reflected well into the twentieth century in the gloomy, introspective paintings of José Gutiérrez Solana.

A MONUMENT IN GRAY

If funerary sculpture is the most representative expression of the "black" mood of the Spain of Philip II, the great monument in gray is beyond doubt the Monastery of the Escorial in the bleak uplands northwest of Madrid—the Royal Monastery of St Lawrence of the Escorial, to call it by its exact name. Built of *piedra berroqueña*, also called "snake's eye," a strong gray granite quarried in the neighborhood, this immense building complex, comprising a monastery, a church, a palace and a mausoleum, every stone of which is hewn with geometric regularity, is a vivid reflection of the personality of Philip II.

The ground plan forms a great rectangle measuring 676 feet by 528 feet; the only projections from this rectilinear mass are the Capilla Mayor of the church and the royal palace on the eastern side. As in the great Milanese designs of Filarete or the architectural schemas of Leonardo da Vinci, this rectangle is symmetrically divided into six sections: the entrance court, flanked by two blocks of buildings, the church and two cloisters. The church, in the shape of an extended Greek cross, has cloisters on each side. In the middle of one of these, the Patio of the Evangelists, is a small temple in the form of a cross amidst the ponds and gardens. The entrance court is flanked by two blocks of buildings, each of which is divided up internally by the arms of a cross, thus forming in turn four small patios each.

The Escorial is a stern and disciplined structure, the triumph of rigidity—rigid in its composition, in its standards and in its form. There are only rectangles, crosses, straight lines and right angles, as if it were obeying rules more implacable than those of a painting by Mondrian.

The outer walls corresponding to this layout are simplicity itself: rectangles with sharp ribs, free of moulding and any other softening features, and severe imposts which cut across the whole massive building as if they were gripping it to make it more compact.

So rigid and austere, so cold and passionless in conception, it seems to breathe the very spirit of the Counter Reformation with its arbitrary demands, its asceticism, its crushing authoritarianism and—it must be admitted—its grandeur, too. The King would never have allowed anything pleasurable, which he would have looked upon as a frailty, a lapse from grace. He was just as inflexible and unyielding in architectural matters, in his choice of ornament and form, as he was in the ruthlessness with which he crushed the insurrection of Aben Humeya, persecuted Antonio Pérez, ordered the death of the good and popular Lanuza, or authorized the terrible repressions carried out by the Duke of Alba in the Low Countries.

JUAN BAUTISTA DE TOLEDO AND JUAN DE HERRERA. THE ESCORIAL. 1563-1584.

The original plans were drawn up by Juan Bautista de Toledo, an architect to whom we owe some remarkable works of severe majesty, such as the palace he built for Cardinal Diego de Espinosa in Martín Muñoz de las Posadas, near Segovia. This palace has large bare, brick surfaces; the only concessions to ornamentation are some Tuscan columns, fluted and rigid, a broken pediment—foreshadowing the Baroque— and some emblematic figures in high relief, all concentrated in the center and forming a striking contrast to the complete bareness of the rest of the façade.

Because of the great prestige which Italian architects enjoyed, Philip II showed Juan Bautista's designs to Pacciotti, who criticized them sharply; perhaps this was why the first builder in charge of operations abandoned the work in 1564, the year after it was started. On the death of Juan Bautista in 1567, Philip did not hesitate to appoint an Italian architect, Gianbattista Castello of Bergamo, who carried on the work until his death in 1569, following the general lines laid down by Toledo. His successor, Juan de Herrera, was also faithful to the original design, though he enlarged it by adding a storey. This very addition serves to point up the fact that the general layout and appearance of the extremely austere lower part of the edifice were due entirely to Juan Bautista de Toledo.

All the monastery's less severe and more fanciful features were due to later changes: the picturesque spires of the church towers (which look like black-hooded figures); the relative agitation of the church, with its three centers of interest, the dome and twin towers, as well as the crowning ornaments, flanked by piers curving inwards, of the main façade. The dark, pointed, slate-covered spires of the towers were a whim of the King's who had seen similar ones in Flanders. Of completely foreign origin, they fascinated the Spaniards to such an extent that they were imitated everywhere and became in time a familiar and characteristic feature of the Castilian landscape.

The church itself was an entirely Italian work, by Francesco Pacciotti of Urbino, whose plan was chosen when designs were solicited from a number of Italian architects in 1573. It is an extremely severe building, with its cold fluted Tuscan pilasters and rectangular apse, surmounted by a dome whose drum—like the upper part of the twin towers—is a rather severe variation of the triforium theme so much used by Palladio. Typically Mannerist, it contains some ideas taken from Bramante's plans for St Peter's, including that of the contraposition of dome and towers which was to be seen later in Rome (in Borromini's Sant'Agnese) and in London (in Wren's St Paul's).

The small temple which Herrera placed in the middle of the Patio of the Evangelists provides a note of pleasant relief, almost as if only the cloisters, a place for rest and repose, deserved such a concession. In the form of a cross like Bramante's Tempietto in San Pietro in Montorio, in Rome, it is not only the "syllogism in stone" of which Lampérez speaks, but an almost joyful manifestation of sweetest harmony.

EL GRECO (ABOUT 1541-1614). THE ANNUNCIATION. MUSEO BALAGUER, VILLANUEVA Y GELTRÚ (BARCELONA).

MANNERISM

In the time of Charles V painting in the peninsular part of the Emperor's domains was a provincial manifestation, and the vigorous realism of the Castilian region and the melancholy lyricism of the Catalan states were effaced by the dazzling brilliance shed by the new art from Italy.

The Master of San Feliú, in Gerona, seemed but an echo of Pintoricchio; the Master of Sigena, of Crivelli; Pedro Berruguete, of Franciabigio; Fernando Yañez (or Fernando de los Llanos) seemed merely to copy Leonardo da Vinci; while Vicente Masip, Juan de Juanes and especially Pedro Machuca strove to imitate Raphael's pure, serene and harmonious aestheticism.

Under Philip II, however, an art that was much more than mere imitation made its appearance: a heightened awareness which shook painting out of its fashionably pleasing, superficial placidity and turned it into a militant tool for making people think and feel. Mannerism faithfully expressed the spirit of the Counter Reformation; it sprang from a desire to sharpen art, to make it more incisive and penetrating, overemphasizing at the same time both its intellectual and its emotional content. In common with the poets of the time—and especially Fernando de Herrera—Mannerist artists delighted in the recherché and the complicated. The more intellectual qualities, linear values, became all-important in the composition of their works; richness and color became secondary. Painting became cold, almost icy; colors often verged on the acid, and the human figure was fancifully distorted to express ideas or feelings. The emotional element produced a type of painting that was romantic, often melancholy, sugary and almost cloying, as in the pictures of Luis Morales, called "the Divine."

The healthy sensualism of the Renaissance gave way to a repressed sensualism. Subjective and introvert, Mannerism preferred twisted poses to the easy, noble and unaffected gestures of Renaissance art. There was no longer balance and proportion, and even perspective ceased to be treated as a precise concrete expression of space and became pure expressionism, often mystical.

Spanish Mannerist painting is represented by a most exceptional artist, an enigmatic figure who came from afar, the Greek Domenicos Theotocopulos, universally known as El Greco. His early training was in Byzantine painting, learned in the monasteries of his native Crete together with some concepts that he retained throughout his life: the Neo-Platonic idea of the primacy of light as a value, the use of color to illuminate and the symbolism of the arabesque, together with the conception of an earthly world of solid forms and a celestial world in which the figures, transcending time and place, have neither substance, shadow nor perspective but are idealized—as if obeying a canon of Lysippus—and presented in an extremely elongated octahedral pattern where the heads and feet are the extremities. In Platonic doctrine the octahedron—with rhombic silhouette—was assimilated to the element air.

To this Byzantine background were added the techniques he learned from his studies with Titian in Venice. While Venice was also a center of the survival of Byzantine art, the Flemish technique of painting in oils had been introduced there and had opened up wonderful new opportunities for development. Having mastered this art and Venetian concepts of space and movement, El Greco went to Rome. Here he could feel nothing but scorn for the flock of Mannerist painters who were imitating Michelangelo, Raphael and Correggio, which prevented him from appreciating the great masters themselves who had given rise to so much vulgarity and spurious imitation.

It may be that he first thought of going to Spain to see the great works being carried out at the Escorial, where the services of many painters would be needed. The fact that his master, Titian, had refused Philip II's invitation because of his advanced age probably suggested to him the possibility of taking his place. It is believed that he arrived in Spain about 1575, when he was thirty-four years old. He settled at once in Toledo, where he remained for the rest of his life.

A great deal has been written about El Greco and the spirit of Toledo, but we must take into account the testimony of those who visited him. From them we learn that he lived shut up in his house, behind thickly curtained windows, and that his library contained only Greek, Latin and Italian books. In fact he was a recluse, and this may help to explain the mutual lack of understanding between him and the country in which he lived—although there were always some who professed to appreciate his works. This was especially true of those in ecclesiastical circles who, although perhaps they could not really appreciate the plastic qualities of his paintings, could feel the intensity of the lofty mysticism with which they were imbued. Though he was rebuffed by the King, he managed to form a circle of admirers and friends and lived in splendid luxury in a magnificent mansion, taking his meals to the accompaniment of music.

One of his first works in Toledo was the *Assumption*, signed and dated 1577, which he painted for the altar of the church of Santo Domingo el Antiguo. This is one of the themes which best illustrate the character of his work, since the Assumption represents the coming together of two worlds, the natural and the supernatural, which El Greco so often set against each other. This can also be said of the theme of *St Ildefonso receiving the Chasuble from the Virgin*. Both subjects are in keeping with the Counter Reformation's preoccupation with situations in which mortal man is placed in direct contact with the Beyond, as exemplified in the many contemporary paintings whose themes are apparitions, ecstasy, martyrdom and final communion.

EL GRECO (ABOUT 1541-1614). ST ILDEFONSO RECEIVING THE CHASUBLE FROM THE VIRGIN. 1585. SACRISTY, TOLEDO CATHEDRAL.

In his treatment of the theme of the Annunciation—especially in the *Annunciation* at Villanueva y Geltrú—El Greco seems to have concentrated all that is most Neo-Platonic in his art on the figure of the angel. This figure, and even more the insubstantial wings, is light and airy because heavenly, bathed in luminosity. Since pure light is unpaintable, at least these celestial beings can be kept as far away as possible from any contact with earth and water (elements which give both weight and fluidity to the earthly figures) and are suspended in pure air and fire.

No doubt El Greco's knowledge of Tintoretto's work helped him a great deal in this feat of transforming the solid corporeity of Renaissance painting into something as ethereal as a Byzantine icon but possessing an illusionary power that the Oriental painters never achieved. Not only do some of El Greco's great works represent apparitions: they themselves seem to *be* apparitions to the wondering eye of the beholder.

EL GRECO (ABOUT 1541-1614). THE MARTYRDOM OF ST MAURICE. 1580-1582. CHAPTER ROOM OF THE ESCORIAL.

EL GRECO (ABOUT 1541-1614). THE ESPOLIO (THE STRIPPING OF CHRIST ON CALVARY), 1579. SACRISTY, TOLEDO CATHEDRAL.

EL GRECO (ABOUT 1541-1614).
THE AGONY IN THE GARDEN. CUENCA CATHEDRAL.

The masterpiece of this early Toledo period is perhaps the *Espolio*, the Stripping of Christ before the Crucifixion, the monumental chief picture painted for the sacristy of Toledo Cathedral. The figure of Christ in the center stands out from the rest not only because of the blood-red of His tunic, which reduces the rest of the picture to grisaille, but also because of its axial position, the flowing movement of its rhomboidal silhouette, and the pathetic light in His upward-looking eyes.

The composition has a clearly discernible geometry, not like the highly elaborate arabesques of conventional Byzantine icons, but angular and yet fiery, executed with a dynamic draftsmanship that is very Venetian and that would be almost Baroque if it were more exaggerated.

It is not surprising that a painter of such power and individuality should be brought to the notice of Philip II. Moreover, it might be supposed that El Greco's mysticism would have appealed to the King's own mystical aspirations. But their tastes and personalities were poles apart. El Greco was all burning passion, while Philip was absolutely icy, stern and implacable.

It is interesting to note that the King's taste had two distinct and almost contradictory sides: while he had a great admiration for the most profane works of Titian, whose paintings of opulent female nudes were sent to him accompanied by lines of poetry, he also had a very special fondness for the works of Hieronymus Bosch, whose complicated allegorical symbolism was eminently satisfying to him. Possibly, too, the strong element of fantasy and sadism in Bosch's paintings helped to gratify his own desires and impulses.

This ambivalence was a sign of an all-pervading absolutism, that passionate desire to embrace and control everything which urged Philip II to try to make the Escorial into a wonderful museum of the most marvelous works of art of his time, gathered from all sides.

This ambition, however, was not to be fulfilled. For the architectural decoration of the Escorial the King had his mind set on an idealistic style of painting, and so he wanted the great Italian masters. But the great Italian masters, led by Titian, declined, and he was obliged to fall back upon lesser talents to paint the frescoes of the walls and vaults of his monastery. Federico Zucchero, Romulo Cincinnati, Pellegrino Tibaldi, Luca Cambiaso, Granvela and Fabrizio Castello, Giovanni da Orlino and Bartolomé Carducci filled the Escorial with Mannerist imitations of the great Italian models.

For the painting of the portraits needed at Court, however, he was more a partisan of the realistic school of the Netherlands. He called upon the portrait painter Anthonis Mor (known in Spain as Antonio Moro) and other artists schooled in the same tradition, like Alonso Sánchez Coello, a Valencian of Portuguese origin, and his pupil Juan Pantoja de la Cruz. It was only for personal, intimate pleasure that he preferred the livelier imaginings of Hieronymus Bosch.

When Philip II decided to invite El Greco, who had gained a great reputation, to contribute a work to the Escorial, he asked him for a painting on the theme of the *Martyrdom of St Maurice and the Theban Legion.* Considering the subject chosen, which was in fact the glorification of an army, and the place intended for it, in the heart of the church of the Escorial, surely Philip would expect a monumental, grandiose picture —integral, stern and overwhelming—with the symmetry of great architecture. He would expect that the human figures would be so presented in scale and lighting as to indicate their importance; sumptuous coloring and heavy massing would be strongly emphasized, and the material perfection of a splendid, disciplined army would be presented as the image of its spiritual perfection. Perhaps, in view of the artist's Venetian background, the King hoped for a picture full of grand-opera effects rather like one of Tintoretto's huge compositions, but suitably shorn of sensualism.

But that was not at all El Greco's way. He believed more in the freedom of love than in the rule of fear. He rejected from the beginning the idea of monumentality which would have made the picture a sort of idol. Instead of conveying a sense of unity around a central figure—although he had done this with the Christ of the *Espolio*— he placed his hero amongst other heroes, to one side, part of the general picture and so more like one of ourselves.

There is nothing stern about these men to make them inhuman. He has given them a freedom of movement and posture which almost verges on ballet. These men could not be overwhelming; rather, they seem to be gracefully suspended in air, their feet scarcely touching the ground, as if they were raised up by the spirit. This asymmetrical composition, without a central focal point, is systematic, as is the lack of any relationship to architectonic forms. The cutting-off point seems to be left to chance, as in a picture by Degas, and while there *are* strong lines in the composition they are not only oblique, as in a Rubens, but sometimes even broken, as in a Picasso.

There is no massing, no sumptuous coloring. A noble humanity comes through its cold tonality and slender, nervous forms: the icy yellows and blues border on the acid, and the patterning is broken up. Here is portrayed no perfect army, but a very human confusion which perfectly suggests the anguish of men who, facing death, are no longer obedient soldiers, parts of a machine, but individual and individualized human beings. Moreover, in the part of the picture where he depicted the celestial beings, El Greco has given us one of his most perfect Neo-Platonic creations composed of air and light, with a dynamically asymmetrical focal point. In this work the artist's thought and purpose have been faithfully translated into plastic terms.

It is not surprising that the King was shocked by the picture. Not only was it refused, and its destined place in the church given to a lifeless Mannerist canvas by the Florentine artist Romulo Cincinnati, but El Greco never again received a royal commission for the Escorial. We cannot help indulging in some fanciful thinking and wondering what the Escorial would have been like if El Greco's brush had been allowed to adorn its walls and vaultings.

It can safely be said that it was in representing the supernatural that El Greco's art was at its most characteristic. That is why, perhaps, it never attained loftier heights than in his treatment of the theme of the *Agony in the Garden*. This is one of those subjects which represent the fusion of the real and the celestial worlds. Not only through the apparition of the angel, but also through the imminence of certain Death, we are made to feel the Life Beyond.

One has the impression that El Greco never gave so much of himself, never worked with so much passion, as in this kind of painting, in which gestures are all-important and form is secondary. The drawing becomes almost like the chart of a passion, the human figure is not modeled realistically, and plasticity is obtained by emphasizing the contrasts of color and light against the shadows. The resulting dynamism lies not in flowing lines, as in the most typical of the Mannerist painters, but in the violent movement of light.

THE GREAT RETABLES

No region in the world possesses such great retables, or altar screens, as the Iberian peninsula. The origin of the retable was in the simple *pala*, or reredos, placed behind the altar. In Catalonia during the Middle Ages retables were already becoming more elaborate, carved in limestone, alabaster and metal. At the same time they grew steadily bigger—and this increase in size was even more pronounced in the simple retables of painted wood.

But in its final form the retable was a fusion of architecture, sculpture and painting. It can often be described as "theatrical," intended as it was to cut off completely the perspective from the church nave, sometimes, like a panoramic screen, extending as far as the sides of the sanctuary, as is the case in Vasco de la Zarza's retable in Avila, those in Toledo and Palencia by Felipe Bigarny, and Juan de Juní's in Santa Maria la Antigua, Valladolid.

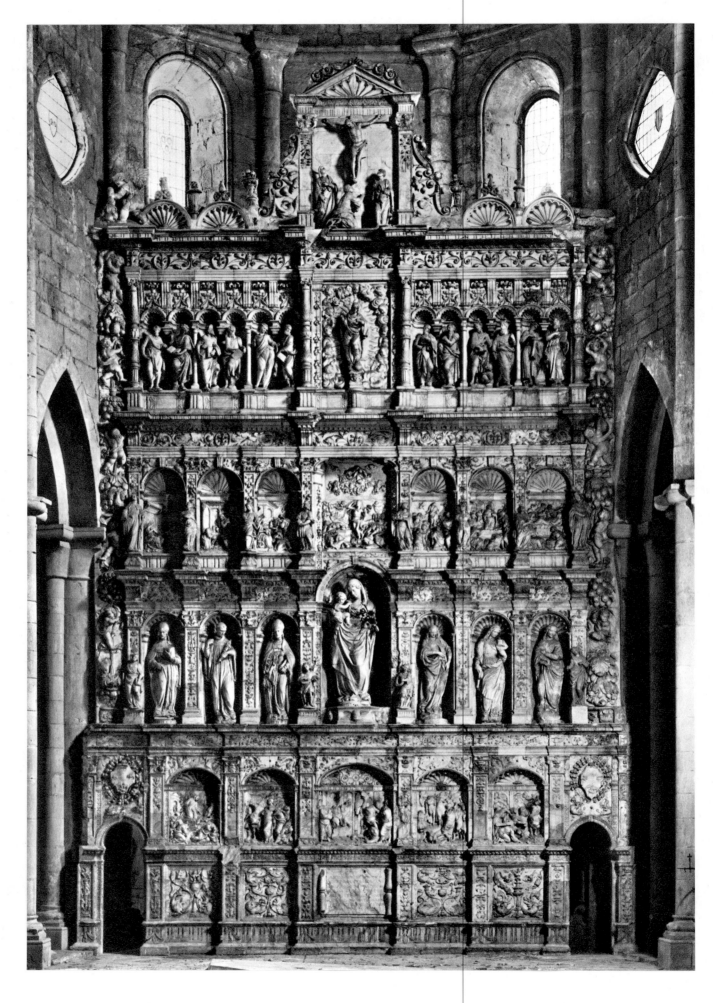

DAMIÁN FORMENT. HIGH ALTAR OF THE MONASTERY OF POBLET (TARRAGONA). 1529.

Its purpose was to attract, to fix and to hold the attention of the worshippers who so became in a way almost like modern spectators at the cinema. An example of this almost cinematographic effect is seen in the Jesuit Church in Antwerp, in the Spanish Netherlands, where Rubens painted a series of canvases to be placed in sequence in the central panel of the altarpiece.

An absolutist church could not allow the private musings and pious thoughts of each worshipper to be concentrated on the abstraction of a blank wall, where they could unfold calmly and without interference. All eyes had to be focused on the altar, all attention had to be captured and systematically transformed according to a pre-established order; all the means of a clever propaganda based on mass psychology—suggestion, statement, repetition, spellbinding—were used to attract, win over, convince and make a strong imprint on the mind of the worshipper.

The most striking example of Italian Renaissance influence on the Spanish retable carved in stone is the high altar of the Cistercian monastery of Poblet, in Catalonia. Poblet—monastery, royal palace and pantheon of the kings of Catalonia—was in fact the sentimental heart of the confederation of states united under the Catalan Crown; not only those in the Peninsula (Catalonia itself, Aragon and Valencia) but also those overseas, such as Majorca, Sicily, Sardinia and Naples. The mixed Italo-Catalan character of the region is reflected in the Poblet altar: the framework is Catalan, not unlike the stone-carved retables in Vich, Castelló de Ampurias and Tarragona. But Italian influence is seen in the excellent statues and reliefs, in the use of classical orders in its architecture and in the grotesques and acanthus scrolls of the decoration.

The Poblet retable is the work of the sculptor Damián Forment, a native of Valencia. Forment had created retables in pure Gothic style not only in Valencia and Gandía, but also in Saragossa. He had specialized in wood-carving, but in Saragossa and later in Huesca he began to work in alabaster and, moreover, adopted Renaissance forms, still within a completely Gothic frame.

He was commissioned to begin the high altar for the church of Poblet in 1527. With the assistance of Abbot Caixal, not only did he design an unusually large retable which would completely shut off the apse right up to the vaulting, but he also decided to execute it entirely "in the Roman style."

We can imagine the shock that would be produced by the appearance of such a showy work—overloaded with figures and ornament, and in a material as smooth and sensual as alabaster—in the bare Romanesque church, where not even the slightest sculptural decoration adorned its capitals, of an architecturally severe Cistercian monastery. We know that the abbot was never forgiven for such daring; accused of misappropriation of funds for this altar, he was removed from office and imprisoned.

JUAN DE BALMASEDA. HIGH ALTAR FROM BECERRIL DE CAMPOS (PALENCIA), NOW IN THE SAGRARIO, MALAGA CATHEDRAL.

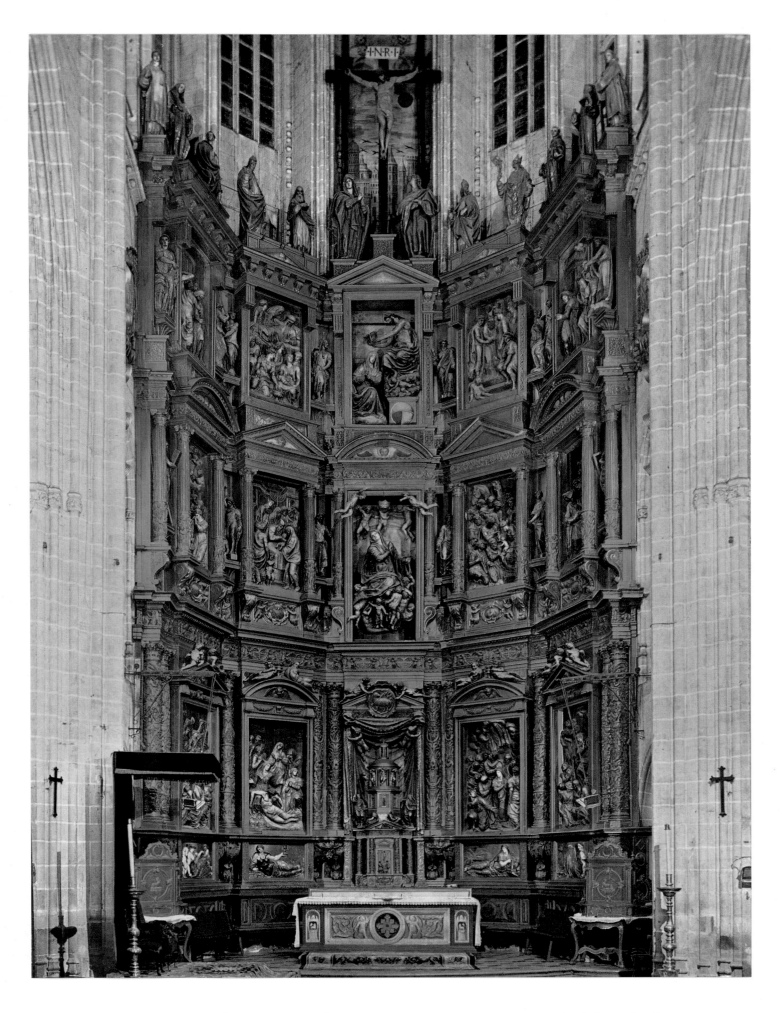

GASPAR BECERRA (ABOUT 1520-1570). HIGH ALTAR OF ASTORGA CATHEDRAL (LEÓN), 1558-1562.

The very spirit of the age of Charles V, with its new internationalism, its discovery of the joy of living, its love of luxury and sensuality, its rediscovery of the human body and noble gesture, breathes through this almost festive retable. Christian iconographic themes are played down so that interest is centered on individual figures, those of the Virgin, the apostles and the saints; Forment has given these figures fine classical counter-balances, serene harmony and restful attitudes. The grotesques add a note of gaiety, showing fluid movement and modeling, good use of empty spaces and a graceful elegance; they are far from having any possible spiritual significance, and the luminosity in which they are bathed sets them poles apart from the dark, shadowy Gothic carvings created by the same sculptor a few years earlier.

The study of this retable, in a region that was the gateway to Italy, serves as a fitting introduction to a description of the great Renaissance retables of Castilian Spain. Here, the transition to a Romanizing style is seen in the retables of an interesting artist, Juan de Balmaseda, who was active particularly in northern Spain. His name suggests that he was of Basque origin. His major works, dating from 1515 to 1549, are to be found in Oviedo, Palencia, León and Burgos.

His unquestionably Gothic training left him with a fondness for minute and complicated detail and a tendency to offset his masses with somewhat loose arabesque forms that have no very clear, strong accents. There are times when Balmaseda's great attention to detail, as in his treatment of hair for example, and certain touches of realism (which bring to mind the mentality of Santa Teresa or, in other aspects, the picaresque novel *Lazarillo de Tormes*) clash, because of their picturesque quality, with the noble simplicity of his nude figures.

These nudes reveal an excellent basic knowledge of anatomy, which alone would stamp him as a Renaissance artist. Moreover, and this is what gives them even greater value, his desire to exalt the human body results in figures as tense and twisted as those of Jacopo della Quercia, somewhat in the manner of Bartolomé Ordóñez, although he never came near the pathetic exaggeration of Alonso Berruguete. Even so, his mysticism has at times something of the Platonic serenity of the poetry of Fray Luis de León.

The sculptor whose retables best typify the age of Philip II is Gaspar Becerra. Born in Baeza, he studied for a long time in Italy, where he collaborated in the decoration of the Palazzo della Cancelleria in Rome with that most doctrinaire of the Mannerists, Vasari. Upon his return to Spain, like Alonso Berruguete he intended to devote himself mainly to painting, and it was essentially as a painter that he later went to Madrid. He entered the service of Philip II in 1563. Under the King, however, he was active not only as a painter, but also as architect—in the Alcázar of Madrid and in the Royal Palace of El Pardo. In the latter he also painted one of the ceilings, a work of historical importance as it marks the first appearance of mythological themes in Spanish painting.

However, Gaspar Becerra is best known for the great contribution he made to the art of the retable in Spain, not for anything he produced while serving the King. His masterpiece is the high altar of Astorga Cathedral, on which he worked from 1558 to 1562, the year before he went to Madrid. His design called for a combination of painting and sculpture, although he himself did only the sculpture. This altarpiece is of imposing size, a perfect illustration of the concept of the retable as a panoramic screen, completely filling the end of the nave and forming a semicircle so as to capture and hold better the attention of the congregation.

It is a very fine example of classical architectural forms applied to a concave structure before Borromini used this device. Moreover, Becerra also introduced other highly important novelties, for example in separating completely the structural elements from the decorative features, thereby giving the architecture a clear personality of its own. He thus departed from the traditional custom of relegating the uprights and traverses of the frame to second place in a purely functional scaffolding. There is a great deal of high relief, with a dramatic interplay of chiaroscuro, very much like a Venetian façade. Thus, what had formerly been merely a system of frames for the pictorial or sculptural features became a series of individualized aedicules—a concept which has precedents, significantly theatrical, in the back walls of the great Hellenic and Roman amphi-theaters, besides the Early Christian sarcophagi of the Sidamara type. After Becerra, this disposition constantly recurs in retables throughout the entire Baroque era, inspired by the same urge to impress as is found in the poetry of Fernando de Herrera.

As to the quality of his sculptures, Gaspar Becerra was a typical Mannerist. Deliberate and lacking in emotion, he had a taste for torsions and distortions reminiscent of Michelangelo, and a fondness for intellectual affectations and an exaggeration of the sentimental. His modeling was jejune and lifeless.

There is no doubt that the beholder who stands marveling before a retable like the one in Astorga would find its modeling insipid if he could inspect its shortcomings one by one. What is really important, however, is the impressive power of an archi-tecture which—despite its severe, classical lines and the monotonous effect given by the strict emphasis on verticality—does not leave him indifferent. It is intensely dramatic, with its interplay of light and shade, and—what is even more impressive—it seems to come forward to meet and enfold him in a way which leaves him feeling small, insignificant and intimidated.

2

THE GOLDEN CENTURY

FRANCISCO ZURBARÁN (1598-1664). ST CASILDA. ABOUT 1635-1640. PRADO, MADRID.

"LIFE IS A DREAM"

The magic of its art and literature justifies us in calling the hundred years of Spanish Baroque the Golden Century, for seldom and in few parts of the world has there appeared such a brilliant constellation of creative artists and men of letters, comprising such names as Cervantes and Velázquez. But from the standpoint of history, in the social, economic and political fields, this designation might be regarded as a mockery in view of the continuous decline manifest at all levels as a result of the fatal clash of Philip II with Europe.

The seventeenth century was one of irremediable catastrophe for Castile. Towns were deserted, silver from America no longer reached the port of Seville, economic life was based on an artificial currency. Throughout the entire first half of the century, the industrial and commercial crisis grew more and more acute, while foreign products flooded the market and foreign traders drained away the lifeblood of the country's economy. The economic and political power of the guilds of thriving industries, formerly a decisive force, passed to the buyers of raw materials, mere speculators, and to landowners who were able to export. Another class of *nouveaux riches* were the spoliators of the lands of the Moriscos, who had been expelled from Spain.

With mid-century came inflation, a steady devaluation of coinage, and at the end of the century a collapse in prices. As a result Castile suffered a reduction of her demographic strength and throughout the century her population continued to decline.

But between the states of the Peninsula, all under the rule of one sovereign, frontiers existed behind which independent political structures were jealously preserved, and this fortunate circumstance enabled Portugal and Catalonia to escape disaster. While Castile was ruined, partly owing to the adverse balance of trade with Italy, and also to the enormous expenditure on its armies, Catalonia retained its credit in Italian markets, made a profit from the presence of non-Catalan armies which occupied it and, avoiding the fiscal pressure exerted by the monarchy, developed her trade and industry. Within the century her population swelled to three times its former size.

The Portuguese, who had been united to the monarchy by Philip II, and the Catalans, who had been brought in by Charles V, were alarmed at the prospect of being dragged to ruin by the decadence of Castile, and sent deputations repeatedly to Madrid to negotiate. The account of the mission of Fray Rafael Franch is indicative of the difficulties they encountered. He returned from the capital in 1615 utterly discouraged, declaring that "everyone amused themselves in card-playing, feasting and hunting, and as for the affairs of the world may they go up in flames."

It was only natural that in Portugal and Catalonia the insurrection of the Seven Flemish Provinces should appear as a model to emulate, and a rebellion to save themselves from the shipwreck of Castile broke out in 1640. As a result, Portugal recovered her independence, while the political and economic liberty of Catalonia was confirmed for another half-century.

In addition to the profound reality of the economic and social collapse, the period was stamped in a still more spectacular way by military disasters, such as those at Rocroy and Lens, by the loss of territory in the cession to France of an important part of Catalonia including the town of Perpignan, the second largest of its cities in population and wealth, by the relinquishing of Artois and Luxembourg.

The seventeenth century started with a weak king, Philip III, dominated by favorites, continued with the calamities of the reign of Philip IV and ended with the plots and intrigues and disorder of that of Charles II, nicknamed the Bewitched. It is not surprising that all expressions of culture and art in this period should be pervaded by a mood of pessimism and that in face of the disasters of everyday life, less import-ance should be attributed to those specifically human values which the Renaissance had raised to pre-eminence.

The Baroque sense of contrast was sharpened by the sight of the mingling of grandeur and misery in the life of the time. The diminutive was admired placed side by side with the sublime, as an interplay of light and shade, the ugly derived value in contrast with the beautiful, the sick with the healthy, the poor with the rich, sinners with saints. On the one hand, a more comprehensive vision of humanity was attained thereby, one into which could enter as themes proper to art, the rogue, the vagrant, the beggar, the delinquent, in a universality which inevitably led, on the other hand, to a deprecia-tion of the former concepts of the lofty and the noble.

The word *desengaño*, disillusionment, is one of the most beautiful and most expressive in an epoch so deceived by life, so stripped of its scale of values that it had come to regard life as a dream—"*la vida es sueño,*" wrote Calderón. Faced with disillusion, there were those who were driven to abandon reality and to search for beauty in the complex, in the artificial, as in the literary cultism of Góngora. Others found satis-faction in their ingenuity in discovering unexpected correlation between forms of expression and the concepts they conveyed, as in the conceptism of Quevedo. And, finally, there were those who, like Calderón, combined in a Baroque full of surprise and marvels both cultism and conceptism.

Although isolated instances of optimism and tenderness existed, such as a Lope de Vega, they maintained a pessimism, or at least an absence of illusion. They harbored an unflattering and uninspiring concept of the world and, at best, veiled reality and its weakness with kindly benevolence while they sought to sweep away all myths, and all idealism, as in the famous satire of transcendental adventures which constitutes the story of Don Quixote.

The brilliant galaxy of Spanish writers of the Golden Century, one of the most impressive in world literature, enables us to perceive both sides of the image of the period. From the absolutism of the Church and of the Court in Madrid sprang the idealistic aspiration towards Baroque abstractions, towards a system of obscure transcendental discourses, calculated to distract attention from material surroundings and to draw the people at large into the big undertakings of the central power, as did the Baroque of the Courts at Versailles and Rome. Meanwhile the bourgeoisie, with their flourishing economic center in Seville, who dealt with merchandise they could see and touch, were driven to the disillusioned realism of the great trading ports of Europe, just as had happened in Naples, Genoa, Valencia, Amsterdam and London. It was only as merchants gradually became *rentiers* that they also evolved towards the more modest and more popular form of the Baroque of their dreams.

THE FLOWERING OF BAROQUE

During the first years of the seventeenth century, the cold Mannerism of the Escorial influenced Spanish architects profoundly. Francisco de Mora, in carrying on the work there, adhered to the pure classical concept in the Galería de Convalecientes, in which Mannerism still predominates; the loggia with a severe entablature supported by Ionic columns gives an effect of lightness and a pleasing suggestion of the Palladian. A still closer adherent to the Herreran style in his architectural work was El Greco's son, Jorge Manuel Theotocopulos, the designer of the Ayuntamiento in Toledo in that melancholy style which the Marqués de Lozoya saw as an expression of the patrician beauty of the twilight of Empire. As this tendency towards formalism and severity declined, there arrived from Italy at the very outset of the century a novelty from Rome, the Baroque.

It should be remembered that Camillo Borghese had been raised to the papal throne as Paul V owing to the support given him by the Spaniards, who had come to know him when he was Papal Nuncio at the Court of Philip II. This pontiff with Spanish affinities saw the full flowering of Baroque art which had found a powerful patron in the person of his nephew, Cardinal Scipione Borghese. The construction of the nave of St Peter's was begun and for the first time the work of Gianlorenzo Bernini received recognition.

ALONSO CANO (1601-1667). FAÇADE OF GRANADA CATHEDRAL, DETAIL. BEGUN IN 1639.

In 1617 an Italian architect from the Court of Paul V, Giovanni Battista Crescenzi, passed into the service of the King of Spain, Philip III, for whom he designed and executed work that can be considered the beginning of Baroque in the Peninsula.

In speaking of the bronze statuary of the end of the sixteenth century the gloomy taste for the funereal prevailing at the time of Philip II has been stressed. It was this same preference that prompted the undertaking of the subterranean Royal Pantheon at the Escorial which was entrusted to Crescenzi, and which he executed with pompous overloading of Baroque ornamentation, in contrast to the frigidity of the family groups in the church itself. Recalling the Chapel of Sixtus V in Santa Maria Maggiore, in Rome, by Domenico Fontana, the Escorial crypt was planned on lines of the utmost decorative magnificence, with a profusion of bronze ornament and colored marble. On the other hand, the irregular elliptical vault and its walls in the form of an octagon constitute in themselves dynamic components which are essentially Baroque.

It is interesting to observe how quickly Crescenzi absorbed the national outlook and to see how he who had been so Italian in his work at the Escorial, himself followed the style of the Escorial in his design for the Cárcel de Corte, now the Palace of Santa Cruz in Madrid. Nevertheless indications of Baroque can be seen here, not only in the new taste for polychrome building materials, but also in the theatrical placing of the staircase extended between two adjoining courtyards.

The first Spanish architect who allowed himself to be carried away by the new spirit of Baroque art was Juan Gómez de Mora, and it is significant that his first achievement was urban, the Plaza Mayor in Madrid.

Pope Sixtus V introduced absolutism as a concept in urban planning. His many original projects were derived from the Mannerist ideas of Palladio and Vignola and sought to use squares and avenues to express the authority which subdues and disciplines a city. Sixtus originated the idea of the square as an expression of power and, with this in mind, erected the obelisk in front of St Peter's and pushed forward plans for rectilinear streets in Rome during the last years of the sixteenth century.

The absolutist French monarch was prompt to follow the example of the pope and in the reign of Henri IV Lemercier designed the Place Royale, now Place des Vosges, in Paris, comparable in its cold severity to the work at the Escorial. With the inclusion of all private houses in the one single plan and the equestrian statue of the King in the center, it is the first example of urban absolutist expression in the service of the Crown.

This impressive square of the French capital, with its colonnade constructed between 1600 and 1612, caught the imagination of other monarchs. Not surprisingly Philip III desired one of equal importance for Madrid and in 1617, only five years after the completion of the Place Royale in Paris, entrusted the building of the Plaza Mayor to Juan Gómez de Mora who carried it out with extreme Mannerist severity. The new façade for the Royal Palace in Madrid, designed by Gómez de Mora in 1619, was another example of the same style.

But this same Gómez de Mora resorted to the Baroque in his plans for the monumental Jesuit house of Salamanca, the Clerecía, started in 1617, for which he adopted as his model a typical Baroque church with its plan of a single nave, side chapels, transept and the dome over the crossing, following closely the plan designed by Vignola for the Gesù in Rome, Mother Church of the Order.

The increasing number of churches on this model, compact, spacious, domed, signaled the spread throughout Europe of the concept of ecclesiastical absolutism. In Spain it made its appearance with the building of the Clerecía, in Paris with the church of the Sorbonne, by Lemercier, and the Val-de-Grâce, by Mansard.

The monumental size of the buildings stimulated the development of a profusion of ornamentation no longer, as in the Plateresque, a proliferation of grotesque decoration but a superfluous elaboration of architectural features, with frames, pediments, pilasters, entablatures, imposts, and openings of various shapes and sizes. All these elements are characterized by broken and twisted lines, projecting and receding surfaces, and are decorated with parallel mouldings, equally broken and twisted.

When, just after the middle of the eighteenth century, Andrés García de Quiñones completed the work on the Clerecía in an overcharged Late Baroque, there was little difference between his contribution and that of Gómez de Mora; so advanced was the latter in Baroque that he designed the oval church of the Bernardas at Alcalá de Henares at the very time—in 1617—that Crescenzi started his work at the Escorial.

Gómez de Mora's predilection for broken lines and wall surfaces gradually developed into a systematic use of placage—the so-called *estilo de placas*, or style of layered planes, which produces a kind of jigsaw effect.

Indications of the approach to this style can be found in such works as the façade of the church of the Discalced Carmelites in Avila, built in 1636, in which the broken line is systematically in evidence. Ideas originating no doubt from Ammanati, such as also characterized the architecture of Salomon de Brosse, are applied here with rigorous geometric abstraction. The design is rigid and cannot be considered Baroque if the dramatic sense of swell and movement of the style are alone taken into account. Such it is, nevertheless, in its essential freedom from considerations of constructive justification and its endeavor to impress, not by the interplay of tactile effects, but by the visual effects produced by shadows.

ANDRÉS GARCÍA DE QUIÑONES. CLOISTER OF THE CLERECÍA, SALAMANCA. 1750-1755.

FAÇADE OF THE CHURCH OF THE DISCALCED CARMELITES, AVILA. 1636.

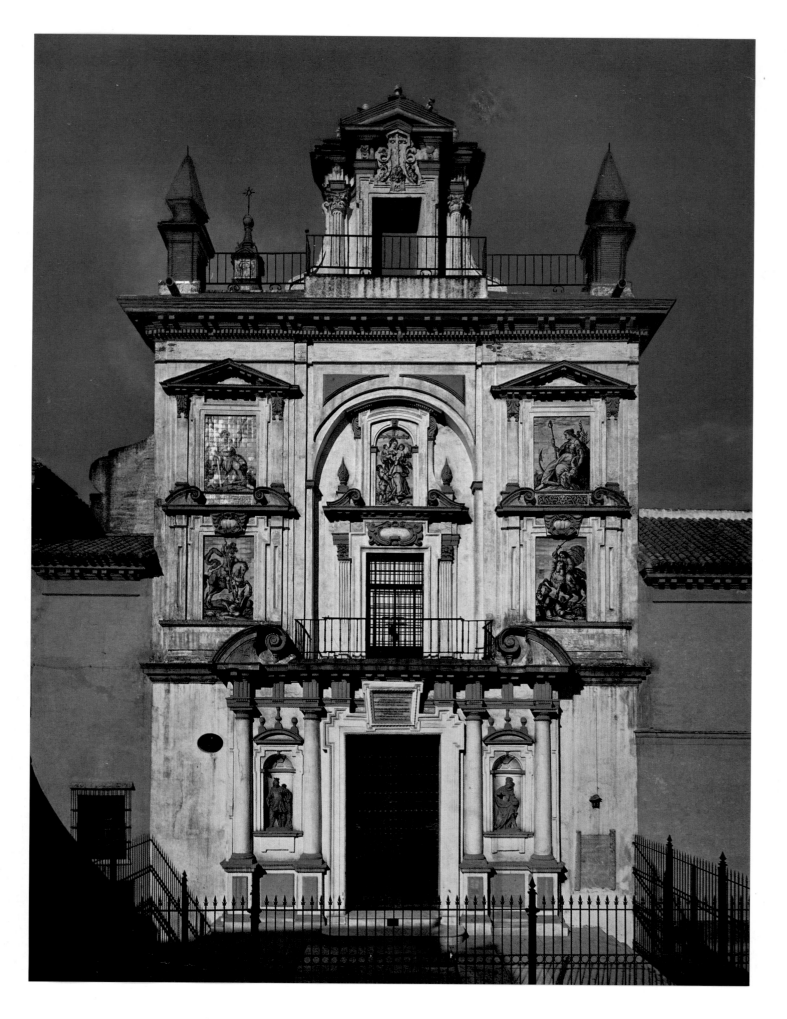

BERNARDO SIMÓN DE PINEDA. CHURCH OF THE HOSPITAL DE LA CARIDAD, SEVILLE. 1661-1674.

95

DOOR OF THE SACRISTY OF THE CAPILLA DE LA ANTIGUA, SEVILLE CATHEDRAL.
SECOND HALF OF THE 16TH CENTURY.

The sacristy door in the Chapel of the Virgin of Antigua in Seville Cathedral is an excellent example of virtuoso craftsmanship and a partiality for materials that are rare or difficult to work. It is a typical product of the heyday of Spain's colonial empire. Pride of place is given to materials at once precious and exotic, such as lacquer, tortoise-shell and ivory, combined with rare woods and a lavish display of bronze that is traditionally European. Works of this kind formed the basis of a plastic style of patterned surfaces, the so-called *estilo de placas*, which other artists applied to simpler materials.

The most daring façade illustrating this interplay of light and shade was designed by the architect, painter and sculptor Alonso Cano for the Cathedral of Granada, on which he started work in 1639.

A general plan which recalls that of the Cathedral of Pienza by Rossellino exhibits a high relief not to be found in the delicate Renaissance work of the Italian architect; it is achieved by three enormous projecting bays which link the four great buttresses of the façade. The deep shadows give the whole a pictorial chiaroscuro in which there is an interplay of lesser shadows obtained by a combination of imposts, entablatures, door-cases, consoles, plain surfaces and pediments, œils-de-bœuf and medallions, all in the same *estilo de placas* mentioned above in referring to the church of the Discalced Carmelites in Avila which had been built only a few years previously.

The visual significance of this style of architecture is frequently emphasized in Andalusia where the combination of yellow stone and red earth, whitewash and colored tiles gives the whole construction a pictorial quality. An outstanding example is the graceful façade of the Hospital de la Caridad in Seville, the work of Bernardo Simón de Pineda, begun in 1661.

This façade is a striking example of Baroque as assimilated and developed in Spain. Within twenty-five years the new idea from Rome had been absorbed and wholly transformed at the same time. In Spain it was not a case of the effect of volumes in movement, the unity of space and mass, the fusion of walls and ceilings, the sense of depth, of flamelike vibrancy, of a projection towards the infinite.

Few buildings in Spain adhere, as does the sacramental chapel of the Transparente in Toledo Cathedral, to these fundamental principles of Early Baroque. Instead of presenting itself as architecture embracing man, as a passionate impetus leading to a mingling, an obscuring, almost a dissolution of the individual personality in the universal, Baroque in Castile, and still more in Andalusia, owing to their own special traditions and constant inclination, embodied a concept whereby solid forms are more important than voids, and the expanse of vertical surfaces in full view more significant than the depths.

There can be nothing further from the sense of the incommunicable conveyed by the tapering colonnades of Bernini than the principle embodied in the treatment of surfaces in Castile and Andalusia, where they are seen as though they presented a vision unfolding to view along the vertical planes of retables and façades, like great tapestries free from any marked emphasis.

The taste for surface ornamentation takes a gay popular form in the façade of the Caridad Hospital in Seville. The brilliant blue and white of the *azulejos* mosaics

FRANCISCO DE HERRERA THE YOUNGER (1622-1685). THE PILAR CHURCH, SARAGOSSA. 1679.

harmonize beautifully with the ochre stonework and whitewash. Pinnacles in the form of obelisks, the bell-gable with its broken pediment, the mouldings, volutes and pilasters, the device of placing the *azulejos* mosaics in simulated window frames as though they were decorated curtains, all unite to convey the impression of a Sevillian entertainment, without any pretension to the monumental style which a Court art demanded, at least for the exterior of buildings. Seville gave rise here to an art of richly animated surface design, of strong visual appeal, suggesting the drop-curtain of a stage—an art in which the heavier, gloomier aspects of Baroque are entirely eliminated in favor of color and unclouded gaiety.

98

Madrid, the seat of the Court and capital of Spain and all her possessions from the time of Philip II, began to acquire the appearance of a capital in the reign of Philip III with the building of a new Palace and of the Plaza Mayor. Here architecture achieved a combination of Baroque decoration with a sense of grandeur and solemnity inherited from Mannerism, and henceforth Baroque became not so much a reflection of passionate yearnings as a manifestation of the love of luxury.

A building which embodies this conception, and which is enriched by the most complete example of the *estilo de placas*, is the chapel of San Isidro in the church of San Andrés in Madrid, for the most part the work of a pupil of Alonso Cano, Sebastián de Herrera Barnuevo, an artist patronized by the Court, where he had been appointed painter to the king. The expenses were defrayed, at the immense cost for that time of eleven million reales, by Philip IV, the township of Madrid, other towns in Castile and the viceroys of Mexico and Peru. Its façade is a colossal order of twin pilasters of composite style supporting a heavy cornice and crowned by a cupola. The interior, the first thoroughly Baroque interior of the capital, is decorated with a fantastic display of stucco ornament, the work of Carlos Blondel.

From this building was to develop, between 1660 and 1669, a highly ornate style far removed from Mannerism, a style which was to appear in the Plaza Mayor in Madrid, where fire had destroyed one of the most important buildings. The work of reconstruction was entrusted to a disciple of Gómez de Mora, José Ximenez Donoso, who proceeded to erect what must have been one of the most daring examples of a Spanish Baroque exterior, the Patio of the College of Santo Tomás, which unfortunately no longer exists. Into a Mannerist setting of frigid severity he introduced a showy design of an almost fevered vibrancy. Arcades of two orders were superimposed back to back, replaced below by double pilasters, and above by *estípites* providing for two main floors and two mezzanines in lively rhythm, the whole embellished by an abundance of sculptural decoration.

José Ximenez Donoso did not venture to introduce so much fantasy into the façade of the Panadería which today dominates the Plaza Mayor of Madrid, a work which rose between 1672 and 1674. Here the stir and color of the Baroque are admirably expressed in the paintings which cover the entire façade; they were made by followers of Sánchez Coello, after designs left by the master, and have been periodically repainted down to the present day.

Castilian Baroque soon became enamored of the complexities of ornamentation which sprang from the same psychological root as those of the Flamboyant and Plateresque styles. Thus it evolved into the manner known as Churrigueresque, taking its name from the family Churriguera and characterized by a spirit of exaltation and disdain for logic and the accepted laws of matter, purely spontaneous creations of fancy.

José de Churriguera, in carrying out his designs for great public occasions, processions, triumphal entries, coaches, catafalques, etc., grew accustomed to work in an unnecessarily grandiloquent and theatrical style which eventually found its expression, not so much in architecture, for example the severe Goyeneche Palace in Madrid (now the Royal Academy of San Fernando), as in retables, such as the magnificent example of 1692 in San Esteban in Salamanca which, with its enormous screen rising to a height of nearly a hundred feet, required the wood of four thousand pine trees.

The transformation of Baroque art in Spain into an art of decorated surfaces may be regarded on the one hand as a proof of the faithful adherence to the inspiration of Moorish architecture. From another point of view, this fidelity seems to be reflected in the whole disposition of space and mass in a building which, though lacking in the quality of its details, possesses an exceedingly individual general plan: the Basilica of the Pilar in Saragossa, designed by Francisco de Herrera the Younger, an architect trained in Italy who here produced his most important work.

Like the *liwan* of a mosque, the three parts of the Pilar church follow each other transversally as seen on entering by the principal door from the adjoining square. Reminiscent of a mosque, and more especially of a Turkish mosque, is the roof with its eleven cupolas arranged in order of hierarchy around the larger central dome. The design of the Turkish mosque is recalled also in the contrapuntal effect of these rounded forms with the slender vertical lines of the bell-towers which stretch upwards like minarets with their crowns in the shape of fir cones. These were built slowly, followed the original plan and were only completed in the second half of the twentieth century.

Another Islamic feature of the architecture of the Pilar is the covering of the roofs of cupolas and lanterns with polychrome tiles in geometric designs, in the tradition of Aragon, a method of decoration of Mudéjar origin which has left so many examples of architecture with tile ornamentation. In the oldest examples, dating to medieval times, can be found an echo of the art of Mesopotamia, particularly of the architecture of ancient Samarra. When the style died out, the technique of colored architecture was incorporated into Gothic and Renaissance structures and became one of the most vital expressions of Baroque in Portugal and other parts of Spain.

Pictorial and visual in essence, it was inevitable that Baroque should inspire painting in a spectacular style. But what Pietro da Cortona, Baciccia or Padre Pozzo designed for the Rome of the Papacy and of Jesuit supremacy, what Le Brun planned for the Versailles of Louis XIV, found little response in Spain. The monarchy of the House of Austria, enmeshed in economic difficulties, helpless or at least obstructed by the internal frontiers which existed between the various states of its dominions and the strife between them, was never able to realize the dream of absolutism which at one moment the Count-Duke Olivares devised and sought to enforce on behalf of Philip IV.

FRAY JUAN BAUTISTA MAYNO (1568-1649). THE RECOVERY OF BAHÍA. BETWEEN 1625 AND 1635. PRADO, MADRID.

The initiative of private individuals belonging to the bourgeoisie in a Seville dominated by money interests was of far greater import in shaping the course which painting was to take, in that they sought a material outlet for their pride and rivalries by commissioning pictures for churches and chapels. In this way, just as their fortunes declined, the Sevillians sought to reassert their social prestige and tried to find in the exaggerated, overwrought, often melodramatic forms of a naive piety some consolation for the loss of their squandered riches and bygone prosperity.

CLAUDIO COELLO (1642-1693). KING CHARLES II ADORING THE SACRED RELIC. ABOUT 1690. SACRISTY OF THE ESCORIAL.

ROYAL MONASTERY OF THE ESCORIAL. VIEW OF THE SACRISTY.

It is for this reason that great monumental paintings, powerful, rhetorical, vibrant, are rare in seventeenth-century Spain, while the pictures of the Andalusian school with their measured, incorruptible realism gained favor and were even to be seen on the walls of the Royal Palaces. There are few surviving examples of the application of pictorial art to architecture which contributed so much to the splendor of Baroque in Rome and at Versailles.

We find a few monumental epic representations such as the *Recovery of Bahía* by Fray Juan Bautista Mayno, painted between 1625 and 1635. The picture is handled in accordance with the aesthetic principles of the High Renaissance, in a style deriving largely from the Italian Caravaggesque painters. It is an accomplished piece of work, notable for the ease with which spatial recession is rendered, and for its varied effects of asymmetry, movement and especially of light interpreted in a predominantly cold tonality in which clear yellows, at times of great intensity, form a contrast with deep blues. These same tones, suggestive of the sun rising through a storm, were applied in the painting of skies in that triumph of atmospheric art, the Purísimas.

A distinctive pictorial theme in Spanish Baroque, the Purísima was perhaps the most Baroque of all expressions of visual art owing to the airy abstraction of its theme. It is an idealized representation of the Virgin Mary as a personage outside and beyond Time, identified with the supreme Wisdom of God which existed prior to the Creation of the World as the Office for the 15th of August proclaims. It takes shape as a figure floating in the air among sunlight and clouds, without a shadow, resplendent, her foot at times resting on the crescent moon, her head surrounded by twelve stars, as insubstantial as a melody, vibrant and graceful. Alonso Cano, Murillo, José Antolínez, Palomino and Francisco Rizi are among the artists who, in treating this theme, struck the most distinctive note.

Of the few remaining examples of the harmonious combination of Baroque architecture and painting, perhaps the most important is to be seen in the Sacristy of the Escorial, that curious rectangular room covered by a segmented vault with penetrations, for which Claudio Coello was entrusted with the retable at the back.

A native of Madrid, Coello was the son of a Portuguese bronze-founder and received his artistic training from Carreño, a fresco painter, and from Francisco Rizi. Juan Carreño de Miranda, celebrated for his excellent portraits, their realism tempered by somewhat romantic, misty tones in the Van Dyck manner, was a Baroque decorator of palace salons using mythological themes. Rizi was a painter in oils and no less attracted by misty half-tones.

Claudio Coello, like his masters, was much influenced by the style of Rubens—the favorite painter of Philip IV, who paid for one of his pictures the highest sum ever given for a single painting. At the outset of his career Coello cultivated a rather showy technique of light, vivacious brushstrokes and rich tones blending together in a dynamic fusion. Something of a virtuoso, he came to specialize in large, intricate compositions giving full scope for all the painterly resources at his command. Towards the end of the century he evolved a more chastened, more severe and realistic manner which makes his ambitious *trompe-l'œil* effects all the more impressive.

Seen as an expression of this idea of *trompe-l'œil*, the whole concept of the painting on the end wall of the Sacristy in the Escorial is highly fanciful, inasmuch as Claudio Coello intended it to give nothing less than the illusion of a vast extension of the Sacristy, as though the retable were an immense looking-glass reflecting not only the architectural setting but those who at one particular instant of time had peopled it. This idea, expressing to the very highest degree the theatrical and visual meaning of Baroque, is all the more impressive in execution in that the artist achieved it without imaginative fantasy. No misty clouds nor shafts of light, nor any of the scenic effects which are so patently artificial in great Baroque decoration. Here, all is presented in a manner so concrete and convincing, including the miraculous flight of angels over-head, that it might almost be a photographic record of an actual event.

The scene represents King Charles II kneeling at the altar with a taper in his hand, sur-rounded by fifty members of his Court, Spanish grandees and officials of state, among them the Dukes of Medinaceli and of Pastrana, the Marqués de la Puerta and the Conde de Baños, and a number of members of the community of the monastery in adoration of the sacred relic, the "Sagrada Forma," a miraculous host from Gorkum which the Emperor Rudolf II of Germany had presented to Philip II.

It is an extraordinary record in which the sickly King, with whom the Austrian line in Spain was to die out, is vividly portrayed surrounded by the personages of his time, of whom Claudio Coello had made numerous sketches from the life. This painting is not only a portrait gallery but a historical document which allows us to observe that on the eve of the great political crisis, when the crown of Spain was to be placed on the head of a French monarch, the proud sobriety and aloofness characteristic of the Spanish Court of Philip II, with his taste for strict reserve and punctilio, had given way to the allure of French ways of life. Philip III and Philip IV had both maintained the majestic and somewhat somber style which had lent nobility to Spanish ceremonial. But the moment of historical decline now made itself apparent in that the way was opened for an influx of frivolities from north of the Pyrenees. The Mannerist mode of dress, which had survived till now, gave way to the Baroque fashion, to the tight coats, to colors in preference to black, and to the airy fancy of frilled lace for cravats and jabots—so many elements which give this painting a lustrous and fanciful touch, all the more welcome in view of the almost unrelieved severity of its general conception. This was a significant concession to the mundane in the monastic Spain of that day.

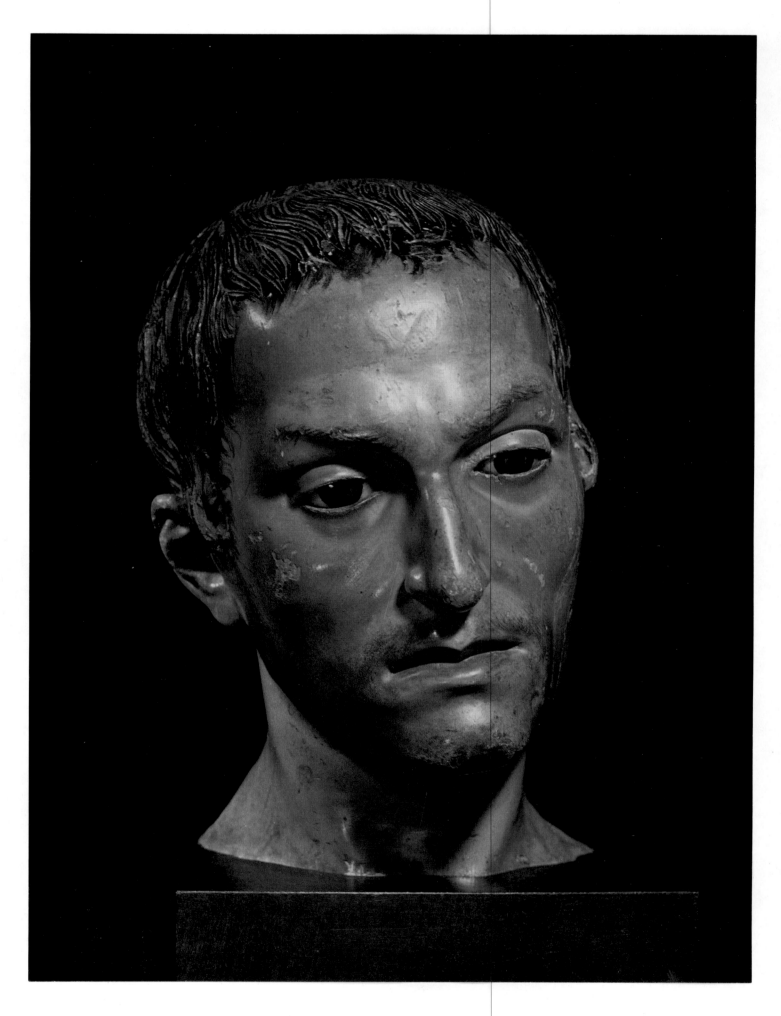

ALONSO CANO (1601-1667). ST JOHN OF GOD. BETWEEN 1652 AND 1667. MUSEO PROVINCIAL DE BELLAS ARTES, GRANADA.

WIND AND FIRE

At the height of the Italian Renaissance, it was no doubt the sculpture of Michelangelo that loosed the winds which were to swell the sails of Baroque art. The same occurred in Spain where Michelangelo's pupils and followers, among them the remarkable Alonso Berruguete, accustomed the eye to its ceaseless disturbance and contortion, to the flickering instability and dramatic content of its high-flown style of expression. But these were not the only circumstances which prepared the way for the movement. As in the case of the Flemish Baroque of a Rubens or a Duquesnoy, it must be recognized that in Spain there existed a traditional flamboyance, intensely concentrated on color values, chiaroscuro, agitation of movement and the arabesque, rising to a culmination of emotional expression.

In regard to this tendency we have already noted, at the time of the Renaissance, certain exaggerated features in the work of German and Burgundian sculptors active in Spain. To a still more marked extent than in their contribution to the new style, we find a kind of pre-Baroque extravagance in the work of Juan de Juní, who was born in French Champagne, perhaps at Joigny (as his name would seem to indicate), towards 1507 and settled in Castile about the year 1545. It was Juní who inured Spanish sensibility to a dramatic expression by means of exaggerated gesture, complicated, lavish and violent agitation of drapery, and spectacular effects accentuated by the use of gilding and polychromy.

In spite of these forerunners, the wind and fire of Baroque sculpture and painting in Spain were usually contained within certain defined limits owing to the Andalusian preference for the real and the tangible, to such an extent that the majority of art historians consider this period of Spanish sculpture, corresponding to that of Baroque in other parts of the continent, as one which they designate as naturalism.

The sculpture of the period is almost entirely ecclesiastic. Kings sought to enhance their importance in the eyes of the people by the erection of equestrian statues in bronze, but this type of work called for a specialized technique and was entrusted to Italians such as Giovanni da Bologna, who designed and executed the equestrian statue of Philip III, and Pietro Tacca who designed that of Philip IV after a drawing by Velázquez and a study of the head by Martínez Montañés. So closely was sculpture connected with the Church that it was largely confined to religious statuary, and in fact to polychrome statuary, for color was of the very essence of the spectacular nature of the images intended for acts of worship, whether in church or in processions. These carvings of divine or saintly personages were made in cedar wood and frequently stood in an architectural setting of black oak from Flanders.

PEDRO DE MENA (1628-1688). THE PENITENT MAGDALEN. 1664. MUSEO NACIONAL DE ESCULTURA, VALLADOLID.

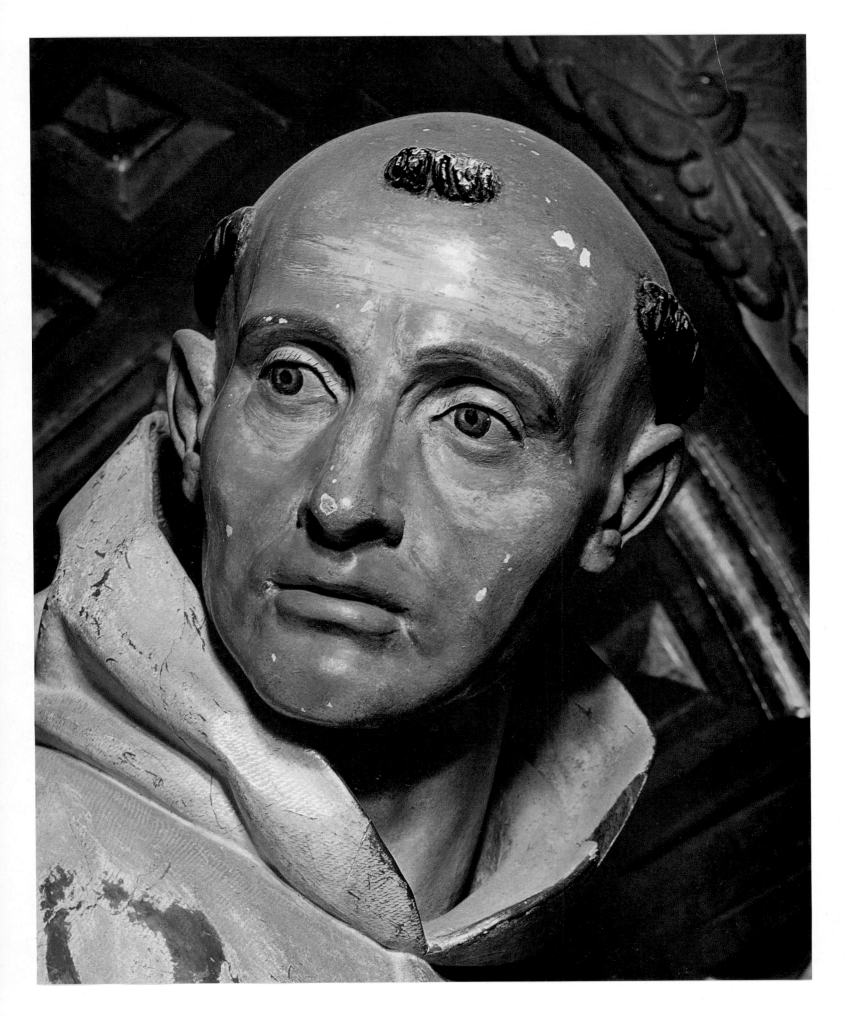

MANUEL PEREYRA (1588-1683). ST BRUNO. BETWEEN 1646 AND 1667. CHARTERHOUSE OF MIRAFLORES, BURGOS.

This style of imagery was initiated by a wood-carver, Gregorio Fernández (or Hernández as it is sometimes spelt), who may have come from Galicia and was prominent in Valladolid during the years (1601-1606) when, under Philip III, that ancient capital was again the seat of the Court. In a world in which Alonso Berruguete and Juan de Juní were swept forward by the current of pre-Baroque agitation and emotional intensity, Fernández represented a backwater in that his conception of plastic art was dominated by an abiding sense of the discipline, severity and formal rules of the Counter Reformation.

In spite of these tendencies, which give some of his works a sharpness and angularity reminiscent of certain Gothic carvings, Gregorio Fernández belongs to the Mannerist school in view of the appearance he gave his figures, like apparitions intended to be seen from a distance and from one particular angle. His gloomy compositions, the *Dolorosa*, the *Dead Christ* which he repeated in many versions, his acid coloring, the cadaverous flesh tints in cruel contrast with the red of the garments, all this was in the Mannerist tradition, but it prepared the way for the pathos of Spanish Baroque sculpture. He also prepared the way for the pictorial element in Baroque by the use of a varied relief in his retables, where figures in the round are accompanied by others in high and low relief, in a scenic complexity which even comprises fluid atmospheric effects, as in the *Baptism of Christ* in the Valladolid museum.

The displacement of the center of gravity of Castile from Valladolid to Madrid increased the lethargy of the creative centers of Old Castile, which had been so productive in the sixteenth century, and was the determining factor in the emergence of a school of Madrid whose founder was the Portuguese artist Manuel Pereyra.

This sculptor worked out his style in the new capital, which doubtless inherited the traditions of Castile but which, from its rigid Court downwards, was dazzled by the legendary splendor of Seville with its romance and extravagance. It is not surprising therefore that Pereyra's art constitutes a sort of compromise between the exaggerated sentimentality of the artistic sources of Castile and the balanced realism and harmony of Sevillian art. This last influence inspired his masterpiece, the statue of St Bruno which he carved for the Charterhouse of Miraflores in Burgos between 1646 and 1667.

It was only to be expected that the Sevillian school of sculpture should become the richest in Spain and the most varied in its production during the seventeenth century. There still remained in Seville something of the vast fortunes which had been made at the time of the arrival there of precious metals from the Americas, and which, even now, permitted a certain social competition in commissions for sculptures. In addition, the lesser classes, victims of the increasing impoverishment, sought consolation in collective acts of piety, the solemnization of great acts of worship, which served to divert their attention from the increasingly painful realities of everyday life.

It has been said that popular enthusiasm for the great religious festivals, for processions and solemn ceremonies of canonization, the passionate zeal shown in promulgating the dogma of the Immaculate Conception, were all expressions of the dynamic force which had been directed previously to business affairs, to trade and speculation. In the now prevailing mood of pessimism, embodied in melancholy and sorrowful images, it was not only the great who could identify themselves with art, as had been the case in the Renaissance; the humble people could do so as well, finding in its manifestations a comforting reflection of their own predicament.

The creator of religious imagery of the Baroque period in this Seville, overshadowed by the decline of its former prosperity, was Juan Martínez Montañés. Trained in classical Granada under the Renaissance artist Pablo de Rojas, he established himself in Seville while still a young man and remained there until his death sixty years later. Montañés was the sculptor of the common people. Observing the faces he saw around him in daily life, he incorporated their features in his statuary, which displays in a high degree the characteristics of a racial type, distinctively Andalusian, with which he had been familiar from his earliest days. But he never descended to the merely picturesque delineations of genre art. His aspiration obviously was to give these everyday figures the ennobling character derived from a classic treatment and thereby to reveal their innate dignity as human beings; in this he succeeded, for his statues do indeed have something of the harmony and balance of those of ancient times.

Exalting the cult of the Virgin, Montañés helped to create the model of the Immaculate Conception, the Inmaculada. By concealing the feet of the figure and placing it on a pillar of cloud, he achieved the effect of suspension in the atmosphere attained by painters with clouds and rays of light. The wind which flutters the draperies of these statues, the heavenly fire which floods them with pure gold, make these figures of the Purísima outstanding examples of pure Spanish Baroque imagery.

Montañés, whose statues were colored by the painter Francisco Pacheco, created an art of highly developed forms and elaborate polychromy which represents an aesthetic response to the idealism of the period of financial prosperity. But as the decay of economic power proceeded, a development took place in sculpture whereby the criteria based on measured proportions and formal balance were replaced by those arising from sentiment and pathos, and appealing to the simple piety of the people.

Juan de Mesa, some twenty years younger than Montañés, has been considered by many to be the first Sevillian Baroque artist, although much of his work was done under the lingering influence of Romanism. However, his most distinctive figures are those characterized by an intense emotionalism calculated to appeal to the feelings of the populace, such as the processional statue, still deeply revered, of the *Jesus del Gran Poder*, its name as Baroque as is its appearance.

Inspired by the *Christ of the Passion* by Montañés, it represents the pitiful figure of Christ crowned with thorns, bearing his Cross. The face is emaciated, wasted, torn by suffering, the hands large and bony. In contrast to the agitated surfaces to which the carving has given a tremulous chiaroscuro, the statue is dressed in actual materials in accordance with Spanish custom. Red or purple velvet embroidered in gold, silver relief on the Cross, light flaming from the aureole, together with the interplay of light and shade, are all elements serving to enhance the impression of an actual presence in the theatrical manner which is truly Baroque. To Juan de Mesa must be attributed the substitution, in his representations of the Crucifixion, of the convulsed and highly emotional image of the dying Christ for the serene figure of the dead Christ.

José de Arce, a Fleming trained in Italy, and a direct follower of Duquesnoy, played a part in this development, and his Apostles for the main altar of the Charterhouse of Jerez de la Frontera were polychromed by no less an artist than Zurbarán. But the full flowering of Baroque art in Seville is seen at its most characteristic in the sculpture of Pedro Roldán, who worked there during the second half of the seventeenth century. An Andalusian from Antequera, he had learned his craft in Granada before settling finally in Seville where he sometimes collaborated with the painter Juan de Valdés Leal. Roldán was a man of the people, and such he remained all his life. He lived in a small farm just outside Seville and would ride into the city on a donkey, shaded by a broad brimmed hat, fashioning small clay figures as he went.

This was the century of opera and the prevailing taste had created a liking for altarpieces with scenic effect, of which a celebrated example is the altar of the Ecstasy of St Theresa in the church of Santa Maria della Vittoria, in Rome, in which Bernini placed his figures within the framework of an architectural altarpiece mysteriously lighted from a hidden source. In some instances this arrangement gave the impression of a stage setting at the far end of the church. This idea was followed by Pedro Roldán in the church of the Hospital de la Caridad in Seville whose façade, decorated with colored tiles (*azulejos*), we have already described. His client on this occasion was Don Miguel de Mañara, a personage of legendary riches said to have been the prototype of the Don Juan of literature, and whose acts of severe penance at the end of a dissolute life might be seen as analogous to the course of life in Seville from the time of the carefree dissipation of riches to that of acute difficulty. In 1670, Don Miguel entrusted to Bernardo Simón de Pineda the general design of the altar, and it was Pineda who originated the idea of giving it the form of a theater complete with scenery.

For this as well as for the chosen theme, the Entombment of Christ, there is a precedent in the performances of religious dramas on this theme, which were given in the Burgundian and Flemish provinces, in France and Germany, and also at times in some of the Spanish dominions during the fifteenth and sixteenth centuries, in a kind of permanent diorama with statues.

These Flamboyant or Renaissance dioramas were not monumental and were usually hidden away in smaller chapels or dark corners, but Pineda planned to convert the whole conception of the performance into a monument, giving it the attributes of the secular theater instead of those of the traditional religious theater of the past. To achieve this he designed his scene as an open space covered by a cupola and lit by a brilliant variety of colors. This was the setting for Roldán's statues.

PEDRO ROLDÁN (1624-1700). THE BURIAL OF CHRIST. BETWEEN 1670 AND 1673. HIGH ALTAR OF THE CHURCH OF THE HOSPITAL DE LA CARIDAD, SEVILLE.

Around the bulky Baroque sarcophagus Pedro Roldán assembled the principal personages of his drama. Beside the leaden-hued body of the dead Christ, Nicodemus, Joseph of Arimathea, the Virgin, St John, the Blessed Marys, and an attendant who lifts the lid of the sepulchre appear to be taken suddenly by surprise as they advance. In this diorama the gradation of high and low relief, an effect already referred to in connection with Gregorio Fernández, is of more importance than in any other work, creating as it does a backcloth for the scene of the Entombment, a landscape in depth in which appear the hill of Golgotha with the three crosses, the two thieves still hanging on their instruments of torture, and in the distance a stormy sky.

Pedro Roldán resorted here to a form of sculptural plasticity which is quite as Baroque as the theatrical arrangement of the group. The carving in deep relief leaves the concave surfaces vague and undefined in order to concentrate on giving the utmost precision to the intersections which divide them. By this means, light striking on the figures sheds its patterns over the penumbra of the general background in a deeply expressive manner. The expression arises from the linear elements rather than from any emphasis on volume. Draperies and beards, hands and hair, caught in this flickering play of lights and shadows, acquire a vibrancy which invests them with life.

The polychromy was entrusted to the Cordovan painter Juan de Valdés Leal, a man of restless energy and violent temper, a thoroughgoing expressionist in the distortion of his figures and the heightened pitch of his colors both light and dark. In both style and temperament he was well suited to impart a funereal character to the sculpture of Roldán, but if in this work he achieved an effect of leaden desolation, he was more starkly dramatic in two other compositions of this chapel, in the lunettes, which were to complete an allegory of Death. In one of them, Death appears destroying Life; the symbols of learning and of human achievement lie scattered on the ground at the foot of the skeleton with the scythe. Still more gruesome is the other lunette, showing a Knight of Calatrava and a Bishop in their magnificent robes, bearing every mark of their high estate while among all crawl the worms.

Francisco Antonio Ruiz Gijón, a pupil of José de Arce, played a notable part in the final years of the school of Sevillian sculptors. He outstripped all the others in his Baroque expression of wind and fire. His figures appear to whirl, to be aglow, often in the grip of intense emotion, as though carried by the wind in a miraculous upward spiral, the eyes in trance. They are like visions and they themselves seem to see visions. Among these the famous *Cristo de la Expiración*, belonging to the church of the Patrocinio in the Triana suburb of Seville, is still an object of popular devotion. This Passion image, a masterpiece of polychrome sculpture, is a work of particular importance, continuing the type of portrayal of Christ Crucified which had been initiated by Juan de Mesa, a Christ represented not in the serenity of death but still alive, painfully convulsed in the last throes of his agony.

Seville at the end of the seventeenth century was no longer the great center of trade with American territories, a trade which it had once monopolized and which had for a time resulted in a strong concentration of capital. Throughout the century it had been declining to the position of a town that had seen better days, in which all that was most vital now stemmed from the common people, who gained in strength from the steady influx of countryfolk drawn into the city to gather up the leavings of the *rentiers*. It is for this reason that the swan song of sculpture in Seville took the tone of popular art, of street rejoicing, with a sprightliness and wit, a graceful buoyancy which has always remained characteristic of the Sevillians, inherited by them from their years of prosperity and splendor.

Granada was different—proud, reticent, more engrossed in the needs of the moment than in the graces. It was perhaps owing to the classical tradition of the Granadine Renaissance that Alonso Cano (whose work as an architect has already been mentioned) saw fit, in spite of his training in Seville, to adopt in all its essentials an aesthetic handed down from the time of Pedro Machuca. Cano was a man of great versatility, as were all the leading artists of the Renaissance, working as an architect, sculptor, and painter. In all three mediums his aim was clarity, order, exactitude, harmony, in accordance with an aesthetic code which owed much to the principles of the Renaissance. His architectural work in the cathedral of Granada bears the imprint of his search for perfection of form, although his use of strong and of delicate shadows as well as that of broken mouldings adheres to the code of Baroque. In his paintings, as in the famous *Santa Inés*, he attains a purity of expression comparable to Holbein. He possesses in general a crystal clarity reminiscent of the Renaissance, although at times, as in the *Virgin of the Stars* in the Prado, he makes play with the misty subtleties of optical grays, after the manner of Van Dyck.

In his sculpture, to which he himself applied the polychromy, Alonso Cano maintained, and often with great vigor, the essential principles of Renaissance art typical of Granada. This is best seen in his *Virgin and Child* in the retable of the high altar of Santa María at Lebrija (Seville), which recalls not only the Madonnas of Jacopo della Quercia and Luca della Robbia, but Michelangelo's *Madonna of the Steps* (in the Casa Buonarroti, Florence) and that in the lunette of the Ospedale degli Innocenti in Florence. The Virgin's dignified reserve of bearing expresses serenity of spirit and peace of mind.

Cano's sculpture also possesses a specifically seventeenth-century aspect in the strain of popular realism which he incorporated in his themes, avoiding any digression into the merely picturesque and maintaining a sobriety and restraint which befitted one who was a friend and companion of Velázquez. To this side of his work belongs the *St John of God* carved in Granada between 1652 and 1667, and now in the museum of that city, an unusual example of the perfect association of modeling and color.

ANTONIO DE PEREDA (1608-1678). THE DREAM OF LIFE. MID-17TH CENTURY. ACADEMY OF SAN FERNANDO, MADRID.

Towards the end of his life, Cano developed a mild form of expressionism, influenced possibly by Michelangelo, and tended to imbue his figures with a brooding sense of mystery. Pedro de Mena, his pupil, testifies in his work to the same desire for perfection of form to which Alonso Cano aspired, and follows him even more closely in his concern with clarity and order, precision and harmony, which in Mena's case resulted in a kind of purism. He would have become the most classical of all classic artists, almost abstract in his search for pure form and purity of style, had it not been that he was obliged to apply these ideal standards to the purely Baroque problem of emotional expression posed by the images demanded of him. He was forced repeatedly to interpret the theme of the Dolorosa, which he habitually treated as a half-length figure or bust. He also became a specialist in statues of St Peter of Alcántara.

There can be no doubt that Mena's apprenticeship in Cano's studio, passed in the execution of works designed by his master, had the effect of orienting him towards a plastic purism which he developed in much the same way as Cano had done, skillfully tempering it with his realistic treatment of human types. This balance was apparent in the fine group of wooden statuettes of saints carved for the choir of Malaga Cathedral, which have now unfortunately been destroyed.

In his representations of the Virgin, in which he kept to the conventional conception of a beauty immune from the marks of age, Mena naturally became more idealistic and sought expression in pure plasticism. This was evident in the beautiful carving of the *Virgin of Bethlehem*, purist and Baroque at the same time, which used to hang in the church of Santo Domingo in Malaga but was destroyed in 1931. The arrangement in space of the plastic elements, the asymmetry of the composition, the play of light and shade, the treatment of the *tondo* as a small stage, are all Baroque, yet are consistent here with an exquisite exactness in the proportions and relationship of all the forms.

Mena's later works, produced in the second half of the century, show a growing emphasis on the contrast between purity of form and expression of feeling. Thus his many interpretations of the Virgin as the Mater Dolorosa and particularly his *Penitent Magdalen* of 1664, as well as his other penitent, *St Mary of Egypt*, are schematic arrangements of concrete forms treated with much economy of volume and design in order to achieve a great intensity of expression. They take on thereby a crystalline spareness, like the visionary saints of Zurbarán, and in the end Baroque acquires a new aspect, archaic in character, imbued with the compelling force of Egyptian sculptures, of the Charioteer of Delphi, or the Apollo of Veii.

José de Mora is another artist who, like Pedro de Mena, came under the influence of Alonso Cano. Last of the great image carvers of Granada, Mora attained the position of Court Sculptor, but died in solitude, in poverty, and insane. Characteristic of this sculptor from Granada, who reached his climax just at the time of the decadence of art in the country, was his ability to transform the harrowing, highly emotive themes typical of the religious imagery which the people preferred, or which the clergy wished them to prefer, into compositions where the sense of the divine is conveyed by a Platonic conception of the splendor of form. In this vein, his most significant work is the *Cristo de la Misericordia*, a "Christ on the Cross" in the church of San José in Granada, executed after 1690, in which the dead body of the Saviour, by the surprising perfection of its anatomy and the exact proportion between its graceful height and muscular strength, acquires the beauty of an Apollo.

The great cycle of Baroque art thus came to a close. Calderón wrote *El Gran Teatro del Mundo,* and the artists had hoped to trace its features in their works. But at the end of the seventeenth century the curtain came down and the love of solitude returned.

THE CULT OF THE DEAD

When speaking of the groups of sculpture by Pompeo Leoni in the Escorial, reference was made to the appearance of that brooding melancholy bordering on the macabre which revealed the fervent absorption of Spaniards in the theme of Death. Death, which hovers round the festive arena of the bullfight, which is ever-present in the popular lamentations of the gipsy song of the *cante hondo,* is portrayed in art in tones of darkness and gloom, at times awesome and majestic, at times frankly terrifying. Mannerism initiated the theme, treating it with haughty aloofness; Baroque took it over and lent it magnificence. Let it be remembered that the first important Baroque work in Spain was the Royal Pantheon at the Escorial.

In Baroque art, almost any theme could serve to evoke the thought of death, as for instance the meditation of St Ignatius of Loyola on the skull. Wind which disturbs all, fire which consumes, speak of life in terms of the transient and the perishable. Statues convey an impression of instability, the fluidity of the temporary penetrates throughout, in light and shadow, fire and water, clouds and shafts of light, all that changes, that passes, that confuses, that hides, and that is lost to view.

Passion became of greater decisive significance than Action. Love denied, suffering, desire, hatred, were all embodied in works of art, as withheld from human enjoyment, in opposition to the spirit of the Renaissance which rejoiced in life lived to the full and drew its fullest expression from the satisfactions thus obtained. Those satisfactions were denied to the men of this period and not only was there a wish for death, but in the very midst of life there constantly came the call to contemplate the Beyond, which the celestial personages, angels, archangels, cherubim and visions of all kinds evoked in the context of scenes from the lives of the Saints.

Among the extreme situations of human and religious experience—ecstatic visions, apparitions, revelations, the Assumption, all of them themes which recur again and again in Baroque art—there is one which has the dubious privilege of being common to all men: Death, the idea or image of which, following St Ignatius, was continually presented to the faithful as a subject for meditation. Death became one of the great themes of religious art and from it developed the widespread popular taste for the morbid and macabre, which in some of the countries of Spanish descent, Mexico for instance, has been carried to unforeseen extremes.

In the midst of vast, scenographic retables and in the *pasos* or Passion scenes which are still carried through the streets of Spanish towns in the Holy Week processions, surrounded by hundreds of candles or lighted torches, and accompanied by men in

JUAN DE VALDÉS LEAL (1622-1690). THE PENITENCE OF ST JEROME. 1657. MUSEO PROVINCIAL DE BELLAS ARTES, SEVILLE.

the awesome pointed hood, statues personifying sorrow and death are heavily loaded with every kind of sensational symbol. Teeth in ivory, eyes and tears of glass, wigs of real hair, garments of real cloth, blown by the wind as are the flames of the candles, all contribute to an alarming reality of presence which evokes a collective hallucination. The pessimistic view of the world, deepened by the demoralization that followed on the economic and political decline of the country, found relief in this cathartic materialization of the darker side of life.

The church of the Hospital de la Caridad in Seville, focal point of a building dedicated to sorrow and its consolations, is a complete example of the cult of Death in Baroque Spain. Behind its gay polychrome façade, bright and colored as a fair stall, the interior breathes an atmosphere of unrelieved gloom. The Entombment in the retable is like a backcloth for the scene, which includes the gruesome paintings of Valdés Leal, representing the overthrow of the great, the enthronement of the skeleton, the powerful figures of Church and State rotting away, in all of which indeed may be seen an expression of protest arising from a popular sense of social justice, of condemnation and demand for retribution.

The author of these paintings, Juan de Valdés Leal, was a true specialist in the rendering of Death and Sorrow, as seen not only in the macabre lunettes of the Caridad church, but in many other works such as the violent battle scenes in the Poor Clare convent in Carmona; in paintings of ascetic saints such as the *Penitence of St Jerome* in the Seville museum, a work of 1657; and in representations of the Passion as in *St John and the Holy Women on the Way to Calvary* in the same museum.

Valdés Leal's preoccupation with death and suffering seems to stem from a conviction of the vanity of earthly things, indeed a repugnance for life, a desire to escape from it or to condemn all that it contains of evil. It is perhaps due to this unrealistic attitude that he becomes at times a painter of fantasy and creates in his pictures, as in those on Biblical subjects, an imaginary world of scenes and cities which could only exist in dreams. This was the period of Calderón's *La Vida es Sueño* (Life is a Dream) and it is not surprising, in view of the moralizing tendencies then prevailing, that an artist like Valdés Leal, and others besides, should seek escape from the hard facts of real life in a dream-world of their own contriving, and find here a theme as congenial to them as that of Death.

The outstanding painter of dreams was Antonio de Pereda of Valladolid, who worked for the most part in Madrid. A craftsman of rare perfection, he combined a minute delineation of details, in the tradition of the Flemish still-life painters, with the over-refinement of allegory and the sophisticated arabesque proper to Mannerism, employing these in compositions of somewhat motley coloring but with a breadth of movement worthy of a Rubens or a Frans Hals.

This strange and exceedingly individual painter specialized in subjects of philosophical allegory, with an emphasis on their moral implications, generally centering on the idea of the vanity of the things of this world. In this vein his masterpieces are the *Vanitas* in the Kunsthistorisches Museum in Vienna and the *Dream of Life* in the Academy of San Fernando in Madrid.

All the vanities and desires of courtiers, flowers and jewels, carnival masks and books, firearms and coins, sheet music and playing cards, tiara, mitres and armor, the painter's palette and the poet's laurel crown, lie heaped on a table in the painting in Madrid; the world globe and effigies of the powerful and of beauty figure in the Vienna picture; all appear grouped round the clock as the symbol of implacable Time and denounced by exquisite and disturbing angels holding admonitory scrolls. These pictures belong to a series which Pereda is known to have painted on the general theme of the "Disillusionments of Life," *Los Desengaños de la Vida*. They constitute a priceless record of the economic and political decline of the Spanish Court and the effort to find a counterbalance in the vehement enhancement of spiritual and moral values.

THE REALISM OF THE SEAPORTS

While the abstractions of Baroque as an expression of absolutism flourished at the courts of Rome and Versailles, a very different concept prevailed in the ports of Europe. Here the mercantile interest in commodities lent importance to the visible and the tangible in preference to the mystifying ambiguities of Baroque ostentation.

The Spanish monarchy in its atmosphere of unreality and disillusionment was unable to elicit any strong support of its prestige, as did the Popes and the French Kings, from the art of their time. Nor did it dispose of sufficient economic resources to summon all artists to its service, as Louis XIV was able to do.

Lacking any artistic expression of its own, all it could do was to attract individual artists trained in other parts of the country, more especially in Seville, where the vestiges of an opulent community still lingered on. But artists who came to the capital from Seville were of necessity those trained in the atmosphere of a great commercial port, faithful to the realities conveyed by eye and touch, as were the artists of Naples, Genoa, Valencia, Amsterdam and London. And this includes a Rubens in Antwerp, devoted to the visible and the tangible and yet so Baroque in his exuberant vitality.

A Philip IV would have preferred to employ great Baroque painters but was forced to accept Andalusian realism, which sprang from roots no less plebeian than did the realism of the Dutch masters. The king gave clear proof of his taste by rewarding Rubens with immense sums for his paintings while keeping Velázquez harnessed in his service at the wages of a barber, which often went unpaid, and burdening him with palace duties which seriously interfered with his work.

Realist art, which was to rise to its pinnacle in the Spain of the Golden Century, was in fact squarely opposed both to the aesthetic of the Renaissance and to that of Baroque. Accustomed to see things as they are, with the lucid sobriety of disillusionment, the realists had no use for the idealized conception of Beauty to which Renaissance art had constantly aspired; and at the same time they turned their back on the extravagant and visionary unreality of Baroque.

Painters were less influenced by popular forms of piety than were the makers of statues, and on this account turned away more easily from Baroque extremes and the pursuit of the marvelous. Reference has been made to the desire of the figure sculptors to represent a popular living type, to approach a portrayal of humanity in its serene simplicity, without regard for the merely picturesque, but it was the painters who were most completely successful in achieving these aims. It was perhaps Murillo, with his richly colored palette, who of all the great artists can be said to have produced work harmoniously combining a devotional and picturesque character.

The source of the new possibilities opened up to painters lay in tenebrism, that Italian movement which enveloped parts of the picture in deep shadow and brought out the reality of the main action by means of an intense contrast of light and shade, thereby placing the contingent in opposite relationship with the absolute, existence with non-existence, so that each person, thing, and object is seen as unique and irreplaceable. Whatever is included in the picture, every living being, every manifestation of the material world, is thus shown in an unexpected light and assumes an unwonted nobility. The tendency of this art is to reveal the innate dignity of all that exists, not by bringing before us things and people of general interest and appeal, but by focusing attention on precisely such subjects as are likely to arouse conflicting feelings. Painters accordingly found their favorite themes in the old and infirm, the poor and deformed, ragged urchins and ne'er-do-wells, and the whole gamut of rather disreputable characters who lurk on the fringes of society—adventurers, soldiers of fortune, topers, bandits, prostitutes, gamblers, thieves, and beggars. In a manner comparable to that of the picaresque novel, the poor were revealed as the truly opulent, the salt of the earth. The racy poetry of poverty proper to a Lazarillo de Tormes and to the picaroon Guzmán de Alfarache enlivens this new world, which had come to dethrone the heroes and muses of historical painting, and which was now to endow religious pictures with an essentially human character.

JOSÉ DE RIBERA (1588-1655). THE MARTYRDOM OF ST BARTHOLOMEW. 1630. PRADO, MADRID.

Philip

2003

The first painter in Spain whose art evolved in this direction was the Catalan, Francisco Ribalta, born at Solsona (Lérida), in 1555. He moved early in life to Madrid, and there had the opportunity of becoming familiar with the works of the Italian painters and their followers in the Escorial, among whom he was most impressed by Navarrete.

123

Whether or not Ribalta went to Italy to study as a young man is a matter of doubt, but it is a fact that he established himself early in his life at Valencia, the great seaport which had been in close touch with Naples from the fifteenth century, and that he was the first Spanish painter to employ the tenebrist technique, his development following almost identical lines with that of Caravaggio—whether by direct influence or by coincidence is unknown.

The Valencian painter José de Ribera, who was trained in Ribalta's studio, spent nearly all his life in Naples and there became one of the greatest exponents of tenebrism. Ribera was not by any means a strict tenebrist. He maintained that light and shadow were the supreme values but it was usual for him to use the gray tones of Baroque, which had been called the sublime hues. There are repeated proofs that his patient study of Correggio in Parma and his undoubted acquaintance with the Venetians enabled him to use high notes of strong colors, especially remarkable being the brilliant splendor of his reds and blues.

In the *Martyrdom of St Bartholomew*, signed by him in 1630, all the characteristics that were to constitute the significance of Ribera's contribution to the history of painting can be observed. It is a tenebrist picture in the sense that it is not color but the use of light and shade which gives importance to the component elements. Nevertheless Ribera shows here that he is not a tenebrist who uses systematically the dark tones of cellars but a daring innovator who does not hesitate to place his scene in the open air and to resolve it at the same time in accordance with the tenets of the new movement. Its central subject, an old man of the people, is the affirmation of a reality quite devoid of any of the attributes of classical idealism. This forthright realism does not prevent him from indulging in a spectacular display of Venetian cloud scenery, rich in Baroque overtones, and complete with Mannerist ruins.

The conscious determination to give reality primary importance coincides perfectly, as in the works of Caravaggio, with a composition which is rigid and even geometrical, built up around a few prominent diagonals, a characteristically Baroque device. Refusing to be bound by the "program" of the tenebrist school, Ribera proved himself to be a fine painter of atmosphere in the Venetian manner. As regards his themes, he handled at one time or another most of those which constituted the stock repertoire of the realists, not even shrinking from physical deformity, as for example in his *Boy with a Clubfoot*.

The contribution of the artists Ribalta and Ribera to the focal center of Valencia was not without its influence in the birth of the great school of Andalusia in which Murillo followed the general conception of the mystical paintings of the first named of these artists, and Zurbarán obsessed by his manner directed it to the contrasts between the concentrated brightness of white habits and the dense enveloping blackness.

Francisco Pacheco, born at Sanlúcar de Barrameda some ten years after Ribalta, was the founder of the new school of Seville, where he spent most of his life. Author of a famous book on the art of painting, *El Arte de la Pintura*, a learned scholar and the center of an academic circle of painters and men of letters, Pacheco arrived at realism by an unsuspected approach. Schooled in the idealist aesthetic of the Renaissance, on which he based his *Arte de la Pintura*, with its pedantic exposition of rigid principles and set formulas, in practice he worked not only in accordance with these abstract doctrinal theories, but guided by the criteria of his scientific knowledge, which led him at times to incline towards an art of direct observation.

This attitude was no doubt a logical one in the Seville of the later sixteenth century where the growing interest in the accounts of discoveries in America and the Indies tended to raise the prestige of the visible, of observed facts, as opposed to the merely theoretical; it prompted the desire in him to represent with strict historical accuracy the setting of his religious scenes. This tendency, together with his official duties as one of the Inquisitors of Seville on guard against arbitrary ideas among artists, led him to reject many iconographic conventions and to study popular types and ways of life so as to give a certain realism to his devotional pictures. The objectivity to which Pacheco had pledged himself could not but exert a powerful influence on his pupil, later his son-in-law, Velázquez, who moreover had found in his first master, Francisco Herrera the Elder, an artist who delighted in bold exploration and novelty.

After these two inaugurators, Pacheco and Herrera the Elder, Sevillian painting found its first great creative artist in the person of Francisco Zurbarán, who was born in the small town of Fuente de Cantos in Estremadura in 1598, one year before Velázquez and nineteen years before Murillo—to name the men who represent the two opposite types of painting practised in the Andalusian capital.

Zurbarán derived his art from tenebrism. Trained in Seville, he may have made his first early attempts under Ribalta and without doubt he was influenced by canvases sent to Seville by Ribera, but tenebrism only partially sums up his work. In fact he is the most individual and creative of the Spanish painters of his time. If he never reached the supreme proficiency of a Velázquez, his art stands out, none the less, as the most audacious and original of his time from the purely plastic point of view, in the formal structure of bodies, the controlled yet dramatic handling of light effects, and the masterly organization of the picture space.

At the outset of his career, Zurbarán was obviously a victim of his own temperament, which must have been timid and retiring, to judge by his three successive marriages to women older than himself—a circumstance which suggests that he felt the need of maternal protection. In the series of paintings which he made for the Charterhouse of Las Cuevas in Seville, this timidity prompted him to depict his personages as

FRANCISCO ZURBARÁN (1598-1664). THE VISION OF ST PETER NOLASCO. ABOUT 1629. PRADO, MADRID.

frustrated, rigid and hunched, with narrow chests and drooping shoulders, their hands hidden or bound up. A man of devout religious sentiment, consumed, one feels, by a burning faith, he found satisfaction in a peculiarly austere form of Mannerism, and when he composed these rectangular canvases in a monotonous rhythm of stiff, rather forbidding figures, set distinctly apart like a row of wooden posts, the effect—despite their often luminous colors—is almost that of a cool grisaille.

These early paintings, in which the composition is governed by an architectonic rhythm very much in the manner of the present-day still lifes of Giorgio Morandi, are already flawless examples of pictorial design, with forms reduced to their essentials and movement largely excluded. Whenever any sense of movement does enter into them, it can be attributed to the influence of the Flemish engravings in which Zurbarán sought inspiration. In his figure grouping, resembling that of the objects in a still life, the direct influence of the works of Fray Juan Sánchez Cotán (which he had seen in Granada) is evident and to this source must be attributed the device of placing figures in high light in sharp contrast to others in shadow, together with his preference for depicting the Virgin in robes of luminous pink.

From the Flemish engravers Zurbarán adopted archaic features such as his persistent use of the broken fold. But from the tenebrism of Ribera he learned to work within the terms of chiaroscuro, and it was this that enabled him to discard his dry early manner and to embark on the rendering of atmospheric effects. On the other hand his natural aptitude as a colorist enabled him to develop an exceptionally wide range of white tones, subtly differentiated, some tinged with blue, others with gray, flat white and ivory, and to work with pinks, purples, greens and luscious reds, handling them with a deepening sensitivity and skill which he acquired through his own efforts.

Zurbarán was already master of all these resources when in 1628 he set to work on the twenty-two paintings on the life of St Peter Nolasco for the Mercedarians of Seville. He executed them while actually living in the monastery of the Mercedarian Order, combining professional work with his religious devotion. This series of canvases—only a few of which have come down to us—was followed by the set of impressive vertical portraits of the doctors of the order, like those preserved today in the Academy of San Fernando in Madrid, datable to between 1630 and 1632. Among these are the unforgettable portraits of Fray Jerónimo Pérez and Alonso de Sotomayor, remarkable for the psychological insight into the character and mentality of these two churchmen, conveyed by the finely shaded mellowness of the modeling; but perhaps still more important is the purely plastic quality interpreted by the archaic patterning of the draperies in rounded relief, geometrical, impressively luminous, in the midst of an enveloping shadow of velvets, concrete expression of a clear exactitude of intellect. Like deeply cut ivory carvings, these monkish figures stand in space, sharply detached from their surroundings.

Probably responding to the wishes of his patrons rather than to his own inclinations, Zurbarán carried out some monumental pictures in 1630 and 1631 somewhat in the manner of the large figure compositions of the Italians. Such are the *Virgin of the Carmelites* at Jadraque, in which the figure floats over a wide panorama of Seville, and the *Apotheosis of St Thomas Aquinas*, painted for the Dominicans of Seville, a work in which he showed a fine dash and energy in the composition as well as the rapid brushstrokes, light as froth, which replaced the studied detail of his earlier pictures for the Charterhouse of Las Cuevas.

In 1638 and 1639 Zurbarán achieved his masterpiece, the great series of paintings which, alone of all his many works for the various religious orders, has remained to this day in its original setting; it is in the Jeronymite monastery of Guadalupe.

Near the Guadalupe river (an Arab name meaning "hidden river"), in the forsaken stretches of Estremadura, birthplace of the American conquistadors, stands this ancient monastery with its rare Mozarabic cloister. The sacristy of the monastery church was to provide the Baroque setting for the series of Jeronymite scenes commissioned from Zurbarán, which he painted in his studio at Seville. Particularly fine are the terrifying Vision of Fray Pedro de Salamanca, the Mass of Padre Cabañuelas and the Miracle of Padre Salmerón, each scene recording a momentary link established between the natural and supernatural worlds.

In 1634, a few years before he began the Guadalupe paintings, his friend Velázquez requested the Count-Duke Olivares, favorite minister of Philip IV, to send for Zurbarán to work at court. The event is highly significant. The idea of entrusting Zurbarán with the execution of Baroque works of art for the court, the decoration of a royal palace with mythological and historical themes, an epic celebration of power, was well-intentioned but misguided; the whole program was utterly at variance with the retiring nature of the devout painter from the remote province of Estremadura, with his limpid, straightforward execution and his intense spirituality.

Zurbarán's most important work is undoubtedly the group of paintings in the sacristy of the Monastery of Guadalupe, which are fortunately still in the place they were painted for as part of a general scheme of decoration, and apparently still have the original frames designed by the artist himself. Though he had planned them earlier, Zurbarán started on the pictures in Seville in 1638 at the time he was working for the Carthusians of Jerez. In the *Vision of Fray Pedro de Salamanca* one monk is pointing out to another the dazzling light cast by a supernatural fire which, though not visible in the picture, is reflected in the faces of the two men. It is interesting to note that X-ray photography has revealed that Zurbarán first gave his monks a more intense, hallucinating expression, which he later toned down for a reason we do not know.

FRANCISCO ZURBARÁN (1598-1664). THE VISION OF FRAY PEDRO DE SALAMANCA. ABOUT 1638-1639. MONASTERY OF GUADALUPE.

FRANCISCO ZURBARÁN (1598-1664). FRAY JERÓNIMO PÉREZ. ABOUT 1630-1632. ACADEMY OF SAN FERNANDO, MADRID.

FRANCISCO ZURBARÁN (1598-1664). FRAY FRANCISCO ZUMEL. ABOUT 1630-1632. ACADEMY OF SAN FERNANDO, MADRID.

Zurbarán's contract with the Mercedarian monks of Seville stipulated that the whole set of pictures of the Doctors of the Order for the monastery library was to be completed within a year, from August 1627 to August 1628. Actually, he worked on them until 1632 at least. The length of time taken over these works explains the difference in style between the earliest, which are weaker, like that thought to represent Fray Alonso de Sotomayor, and the later ones, like the portrait of Fray Jerónimo Pérez. Other differences may be due to the hand of Zurbarán's assistant, Francisco Reina.

Fray Francisco Zumel, one of the most famous Thomist philosophers of the sixteenth century, was professor at the University of Salamanca and General of the Order. He was also counsellor to Philip II and Philip III.

Fray Jerónimo Pérez was a famous theologian who taught at the Universities of Valencia and Salamanca in the sixteenth century. He wrote a commentary on St Thomas Aquinas. This portrait was not painted from life, but is an imaginary likeness.

The third portrait, unlike the others, bears no inscription. The Marquis of Saltillo identified the sitter as Fray Alonso de Sotomayor, General of the Order and Archbishop of Oristano, in Sardinia, who was also painted by Valdés Leal.

Fray Hernando de Santiago was a famous preacher whom Philip II called "Golden Lips," in admiration of his eloquence. He was born in Seville and became Rector of the College of San Laureano. This picture is marked "vera efigie" (true likeness), indicating that it is a genuine portrait, painted from life.

He was named Painter to the King and carried out for the Hall of the Realms in the Buen Retiro Palace the series of the *Labors of Hercules* and the *Relief of Cadiz*, but these works inevitably were a failure. His rugged austerity was incompatible with the operatic staging with full orchestra necessary for such a task. The best part of these paintings is to be found in the enchanting landscape vistas in the backgrounds, legendary, imaginative, enlivened with waterfalls inspired no doubt by Flemish engravings or the painting of Patinir which Zurbarán would have seen in the Palace in Madrid.

His short stay in Madrid, with its opportunity of studying the paintings in the royal collection, contributed to his development, nevertheless, as can be seen in the graceful demeanor of his female figures such as the *St Casilda* in the Prado, the *St Apollonia* in the Louvre, and the ancient Sibyls in the Hospital de la Sangre in Seville. These pictures belong to the period in the latter half of the 1630s when, working for the Charterhouse of Jerez de la Frontera, he painted the series of single saints, each one walking as in a procession, among them the very realistic portrait of *Blessed John Houghton*. They follow one another along a curved passage of the Charterhouse on the way to the Sagrario in which angelic censor-bearers, curiously immaterial and transparent, as though of glass or ice, flank the entrance to a fabulous shrine paved with silver.

THE DISCOVERY OF THE OBJECT

Prompted by the interest of merchants in their goods, the middle classes were gradually led to take an interest in objects for their own sake, as represented by artists. What had been of secondary importance in medieval painting, including that of the Renaissance, and rejected as out of keeping with the Grand Opera style that prevailed in the large figure compositions of Baroque murals, now became an essential ingredient of the easel pictures executed for a bourgeois clientèle.

Things, precious or domestic, decorative or useful, were the focus, the chief center of interest of a new kind of picture which became a speciality of seventeenth-century Spanish painting. This was the *bodegón*, a still-life display of food (fruit, fowl, fish, etc.), sometimes including figures.

The still life, for the first time in the history of European art, gave prominence to purely material values. It served to define the significant antithesis of grandeur and poverty, a paramount factor in the moral considerations of the time; and it also brought home the instructive paradox that small and trivial things may have a

FRANCISCO ZURBARÁN (1598-1664). STILL LIFE, DETAIL. PRADO, MADRID. (FROM THE CAMBÓ COLLECTION).

FRANCISCO ZURBARÁN (1598-1664). STILL LIFE. PRADO, MADRID (FROM THE CAMBÓ COLLECTION).

grandeur of their own. Here was a discovery that in effect added a new dimension to painting. It was perhaps an inevitable consequence of the spread of realism that artists should now be led to focus their attention on almost any object that came to hand, natural or man-made, a piece of fruit or a fine vase, a shabby object or a sumptuous one, in order to convey the fullness of being inherent in every created thing. The part played in this type of painting by sheer virtuosity must not be overlooked, nor the pleasure taken by kings and courtiers in assessing the artist's ability to achieve illusionist effects of *trompe-l'œil*, to reproduce the quality of the materials, fruit, furs, metals, glass, flowers, textiles. Nor the vanity of bourgeois and sovereigns alike which found satisfaction in the representation, almost the portraiture, of the precious things which belonged to them, a proud and public assertion of their wealth.

The influence of the Flemish school was to be paramount in the adoption of this new pictorial theme, which, it seems, was practised in Spain for the first time by a painter of Madrid, Juan van der Hamen, son and pupil of a Flemish painter.

But the Spanish still life, which was destined to evolve in the surroundings of bourgeois culture in Andalusia prior to its development in the capital, took in the hands of Andalusian painters a form very different from the prodigal display of opulence which characterized the highly complex, fully Baroque still lifes of the Flemish masters. The real initiator of the Spanish style of still-life painting was the Carthusian monk, Fray Juan Sánchez Cotán, born at Alcázar de San Juan, near Toledo, in 1561. After being trained as a painter in Toledo, he took orders and resided at the Charterhouse in Granada from 1612 to the year of his death, 1627. To this period in Granada must be assigned his famous *Still Life with a Cardoon*, one of the fundamental works of Spanish painting, now in the Granada museum; there are replicas in Madrid (Prado and Collection of the Duke of Hernani). It is an extraordinary creation for an artist whose rendering of figures is apt to be severe, rugged, and rather ponderous. His

FRAY JUAN SÁNCHEZ COTÁN (1561-1627). STILL LIFE WITH A CARDOON. AFTER 1612. MUSEO PROVINCIAL DE BELLAS ARTES, GRANADA.

ascetic severity, resembling that of Zurbarán, and deriving possibly from his analytical mind and temperamental reserve, underlies the strict precision of the painting and, together with the absence of all embellishment and ostentation, sets it in the category of pure plastic art, immune from the superficial features of Flemish still lifes.

It is recognized that Zurbarán, doubtless sent to the Charterhouse in Granada by his Carthusian friends in Seville, was strongly influenced by the work of Fray Sánchez Cotán. It is therefore not surprising that he followed the same principles as his predecessor and accepted a conception of existence expressed in the purely pictorial terms of rhythm, volume, contour, material quality, light and shade.

The most famous of these creations of Zurbarán, the still life presented to the Prado by Francisco Cambó, builds up a calm and sober tracery of rhythms in which slender intersected forms alternate with swelling rounded ones. The ovals of the dishes create a symmetrical pattern and the varying heights of the objects suggest four notes of music. The color scheme, of the utmost simplicity and harmony, consists of the gilt bronze of the goblet and the silvery tones of the dish, the red of one of the vases and the white of the other two, one dull, the other shining. It is easy to understand the affection felt by Velázquez, lover of humanity, for his friend Zurbarán, whose simplicity and integrity, opposed to all ostentation, has remained an unblemished heritage of Spain's Golden Century.

THE HUMAN TOUCH

It sometimes happens, by a seeming paradox, that what appear to be the most unfavorable circumstances for the development of the human personality actually give rise, either by reaction or the natural bias of contrasts, to some decisive advance in man's way towards a better understanding of himself and his fellow men.

Thus it is that the Spanish scene during the Golden Century, as it has been called, a period so disastrous for the economy, the social structure, the political system and the ideological superstructure of the country, contains a feature of the utmost importance for the history of civilization: a growing recognition of human values. It should suffice to recall that this is the age of Cervantes, the man who proclaimed the inadequacy of the irrational romantic ideas of his world, at a time when scientific progress and the practical organization of labor and of economic life were about to produce momentous changes in the rest of Europe.

For Cervantes realized that those around him in authority lived in a dream world, unconnected with reality, and that the people paid through suffering and poverty, exploitation and cruelty, for the total impracticability of the ideas with which their leaders thought to cope with the inexorable conditions of the material world. Perhaps Cervantes was ambiguous since he did not make it quite clear whether this Quixotic idealism, blind to reality, was an admirable thing, or whether it was not sheer lunacy to fail to base life on the acceptance of actual facts, even though these be coarse or nasty or disagreeable. His irony was relative, to say the least, and this simple relativity carried within it the germ of dissolution of all absolutism and the fertile seed from which sprang the aspiration towards liberty and the equality of man.

That which Cervantes initiated at the turn of the sixteenth and seventeenth centuries, Velázquez carried forward during the first half of the seventeenth, with an insight and a quiet self-assurance on a par with his exceptional genius. Diego Rodríguez de Silva y Velázquez was born at Seville in 1599, of mixed Portuguese and Andalusian descent. He had the good fortune to find in the city of his birth a stimulating atmosphere of intellectual freedom and open-mindedness, far removed from the hidebound absolutism of the court. Pupil and later son-in-law of Francisco Pacheco, a Romanist in theory but a realist in practice, Velázquez resolved his master's conflict in favor of realism, so much so that when it was suggested that instead of painting commonplace still lifes he should use his prodigious gifts to paint scenes comparable with those of Raphael, he replied that he preferred to be foremost in the commonplace rather than second in such refinements. The tenebrism of Ribera, whose paintings were beginning to reach Seville about this time, still further encouraged him to practise and master the realism he had learned from Pacheco. His early works, such as the *Old Woman Frying Eggs* and the *Water Carrier of Seville*, accordingly made their appearance conditioned by the laws of contrasting light and shade.

The knowledge of Italian painting which he gained from a visit to the royal collections in Madrid, in 1622, had an almost immediate effect on his style. It brought about a softening of the rather hard outlines of his early pictures; it awakened his natural sensitiveness to atmosphere and developed his aptitude for the rendering of cloud effects and the airiness of space. When Velázquez was called to the court in 1623, both King Philip IV and his all-powerful minister the Count-Duke Olivares were astounded by his talent, and fell at once under the spell of his art. Though perhaps incapable of perceiving the deeper significance of his work, they could appreciate his exceptional powers as a portraitist, his ability to obtain with a few light assured strokes of his brush a likeness full of vitality and expressiveness.

Within a few months after his arrival in Madrid, Velázquez was placed on the royal pay-roll—attached to the royal household at a barber's salary in the capacity of an usher. Not that we may suppose from this that Philip IV would ever have ventured to compare his painting, acquired thus at so low a cost, to that of the pompous Rubens whom he valued so highly. It is not difficult to understand the social position in which Velázquez was placed and its effect upon him, when we reflect that henceforth he sought urgently to gain acceptance into the Order of Santiago which would automatically place him on a footing of equality with the nobility, possessors of all privilege. In 1628, while Velázquez was living in the palace as an attendant in the royal household, Rubens was received there with every mark of respect and commissioned to paint the sovereigns, the princes and infantas, portraits destined to be sent to their royal relatives throughout Europe. The work carried out by Velázquez at that time, the *Triumph of Bacchus*, also called *The Topers*, was considered no more than an amusement for the court, the record of a pantomime by the servants.

In 1629 Velázquez made his first journey to Italy where he painted two large, rather dry historical and mythological pictures, the *Bloody Coat of Joseph* and the *Forge of Vulcan*. As Court Painter on his return, from 1631 onwards, he was tireless in painting portraits of the King and Queen, of the princes and the highly-placed, as well as of the court jester Pablillos. He received commissions for monumental historical paintings such as the *Surrender of Breda*, the famous picture known as *The Lances*, but his preference was always for the court dwarfs and buffoons.

Each of these paintings reveals the inner attitude of an artist who could turn the record of a victorious battle into the portrayal of the gracious bearing of a conqueror honoring a respected enemy; an artist who could portray dwarfs and idiots with unflinching truthfulness, yet in a way that inspires neither disgust nor commiseration, so human, so tactful and comprehending is his approach to them. Indeed these portraits are a noble testimonial to his respect for and understanding of his fellow men, whatever their physical or mental afflictions. He discerns and brings home to us the spiritual nobility of these unfortunates, thereby confounding our pride and pretensions as effectively as the irony of Cervantes had done.

On the other hand, royal personages and the proud swaggering Count-Duke Olivares are portrayed as unidealized human beings, all their fatuity plain to see. Nor does Velázquez in any way flatter the unruly pope, Innocent X, whom he painted at Rome in 1650 during his second journey to Italy.

Velázquez painted this canvas about 1634 as an overdoor panel for the Hall of the Realms in the Buen Retiro Palace. It represents the young Prince on horseback, wearing a black felt hat, a cloth of gold doublet with lace collar, and green velvet breeches embroidered in gold. He also has a general's sash and baton. From the Buen Retiro, the picture went to the New Palace and from there to the Prado.

DIEGO VELÁZQUEZ (1599-1660). EQUESTRIAN PORTRAIT OF PRINCE BALTASAR CARLOS. ABOUT 1634. PRADO, MADRID.

DIEGO VELÁZQUEZ (1599-1660). THE TAPESTRY WEAVERS. 1657. PRADO, MADRID.

This picture was painted about 1657 for the Buen Retiro Palace. It represents the interior of the Santa Isabel tapestry factory in Madrid, which specialized in restoring and repairing tapestries rather than weaving new works. At the time the director was Juan Alvarez, a master tapestry-maker and protégé of José Nieto Velázquez, the painter's relative who appears in the *Maids of Honor*.

The women in the penumbra of the foreground are spinning and winding yarn; behind them, in a well-lit sales-room at the back, three ladies are examining a tapestry with a mythological subject on which we can see the figures of Juno and Minerva.

DIEGO VELÁZQUEZ (1599-1660). THE INFANTA MARIA TERESA. ABOUT 1653. KUNSTHISTORISCHES MUSEUM, VIENNA.

DIEGO VELÁZQUEZ (1599-1660). THE INFANTA MARGARITA OF AUSTRIA. ABOUT 1660. KUNSTHISTORISCHES MUSEUM, VIENNA.

DIEGO VELÁZQUEZ (1599-1660). THE INFANTA MARGARITA. ABOUT 1656. KUNSTHISTORISCHES MUSEUM, VIENNA.

SPACE, AIR AND LIGHT

It has been said that Velázquez is all smoldering ardor and contained passion, concentrated virility and spirited gracefulness; that everything to which he put his hand is imbued with a lofty, punctilious and melancholy elegance. It has been said that he was a man of a pessimistic turn of mind; that his was an aesthetic of the "salvation of the individual," an aesthetic whose greatness lies in its power of conveying to us the profound and unique poetry of all that met his eye; and that in his painting man and beast, mountains and twilights, saints and madmen, are tinged with the melancholy gravity of a contemplative spirit that accepted the world religiously, in its entirety, loving and reverencing life in all its forms.

His respect for and love of others arose not from any sense of weakness but from the reasoned control of his own strength. Free from illusions, with a lucid awareness of human limitations, he had that unfettered vision of nature which sees things "steadily and whole"; he discerned their intrinsic poetry and this took the place in his mind of deceptive ideals. The universality of this point of view gave him an abiding sense of fellowship with all things and beings. And the result of this egalitarian tolerance was a contempt for the empty pride which dressed itself in heroism, a repugnance for the self-sufficiency of those who deem themselves wise, who maintain that there are innate superiorities and inferiorities between men; hence his rooted aversion to any kind of self-assertion, to anything in the way of arrogance or presumption.

A close parallel can be drawn between each of the terms in this enumeration of moral attitudes and the techniques employed in his art. Moral strength is revealed in the absolute assurance of his brushwork, in the judicious placing of figures in a composition; self-control in his consistent avoidance of the spirited but showy execution of a Frans Hals and the surging expressionism of a Rubens. Freedom from illusion prevented him from becoming involved in the superficial representation of outward semblances. The figures in his palace portraits were divested of majesty, the divine was stripped of mysticism, mythology of its literary associations, and prejudice against the poor and the abnormal was cleared away. On this basis, there was no place in his art for theatrical effects, strained or contorted movements, the fluttering draperies and soaring figures of Baroque, Olympian lights, or anything rhetorical or pompous. Without artifice or superfluity, all is simplicity and due proportion.

The all-embracing simplicity and truthfulness of his vision rules out any conventional hierarchy in his portrayal of people. All men are brothers, none takes precedence over others, as had been the case in the pyramidal compositions of the Renaissance; nor is anyone relegated to one side, as in the oblique alignments of Baroque art. In his eyes

DIEGO VELÁZQUEZ (1599-1660). THE MAIDS OF HONOR. 1656. PRADO, MADRID.

DIEGO VELÁZQUEZ (1599-1660). THE INFANTA MARGARITA IN A BLUE GOWN. ABOUT 1659. KUNSTHISTORISCHES MUSEUM, VIENNA.

This sketch of Granada Cathedral and the surrounding houses is interesting on two counts: first, that very few drawings by Velázquez are extant and, secondly, that works by him in which there are no human figures are relatively rare.

Of all Velázquez's paintings, the one most closely related to this drawing is the famous *View of Saragossa* executed in collaboration with his son-in-law Mazo, and now in the Prado. Mazo is usually credited with all the architectural part of the picture and Velázquez is thought to have been responsible only for the figures which animate the view of the city from across the river. This is the traditional thesis, propounded emphatically by Beruete, who supposes that Velázquez did the numerous groups in the foreground, along the river bank, and Mazo the buildings behind, since the former was a great figure painter and the latter was reputed for his panoramas, hunting scenes and town views.

Sánchez Cantón, on the contrary, has suggested a diametrically opposite attribution. In his eyes, the figures should be assigned to Mazo because of their anecdotal, picturesque nature, whereas the atmosphere enveloping the buildings demands a knowledge of space that Velázquez alone possessed. Lafuente Ferrari also believes that Velázquez took a hand in the architectural part of the *View of Saragossa*.

These assertions are borne out by this *View of Granada* in which Velázquez has rendered with characteristic simplicity and an engaging liveliness the atmosphere, the light, and the air that circulates among the roofs.

DIEGO VELÁZQUEZ (1599-1660). VIEW OF GRANADA. SEPIA DRAWING. BIBLIOTECA NACIONAL, MADRID.

the court jester Calabacillas is as worthy of attention as the Count-Duke Olivares, the triumphant Bacchus as the garlic, eggs and fish of *Christ in the House of Mary and Martha*. This moral impartiality is reflected in the quiet, unemphatic distribution of values and tones, devoid of any shrill note or accents, in a harmonious blending of colors which is the very essence of the graceful refinement, even temper and good breeding which characterize all his work.

The more familiar we become with the paintings of Velázquez, the more certain we are to realize that their true content lies not in the subject matter itself, which only acts as a kind of *collage*, but rather in the ensemble of forms which go to express his attitude to life. Bearing this in mind, we may observe two features which recur again and again in his pictures: the empty central space and the gesture of the hand.

The center of the picture space was never left unoccupied in Renaissance painting but always held the main figure or group of figures, which thus formed the hub of the composition, in keeping with the Renaissance practice of centering everything on man. Mannerist architecture, however, made use of the central void, the reason being that this center was designed for occupation by a human figure. Following Michelangelo, it was developed by such Italian architects as Palladio, Vasari, Vignola and Rainaldi in San Giorgio Maggiore (Venice), in the Uffizi (Florence), and in the Villa of Pope Julius and the Piazza del Popolo (Rome). This transformation of the center from its Renaissance purpose as framework to the subjects of the composition, into a space around which these subjects are situated, is one of the most decisive aspects of the process whereby Velázquez did away with hierarchies and invidious discrimination, laying the emphasis on ultimate values far removed from visible hierarchies and located rather in an invisible distance, tending towards unknown ends.

In some of the early works, as in the *Christ in the House of Mary and Martha*, the perspective recession is given added depth by an opening at the back, in the form of a window. But already in the *Triumph of Bacchus* the theme of the empty central space begins to appear in the shape of a cleavage dividing the figure group in two. The same central division occurs in the *Forge of Vulcan*, while in the *Surrender of Breda* it is clearly developed in the hexagonal space which forms the focal point of the composition and contains the symbol of its meaning, the handing over of the keys to the city.

This deeply receding void in the center of the picture is still more skillfully treated in the *Maids of Honor*, where the unreality of the space reflected in the mirror intervenes, as it does again in the *Rokeby Venus*. In the *Tapestry Weavers*, on the other hand, this emptiness is conveyed by the disquieting presence of a small round window communicating with an undefined area of darkness, while through invisible windows in the foreground stream rays of bright sunlight, image of the joys of life distracting our eye from the destiny ever awaiting us.

DIEGO VELÁZQUEZ (1599-1660). THE COURT JESTER CALABACILLAS ("THE IDIOT OF CORIA"). BEFORE 1639. PRADO, MADRID.

The persistent recurrence of this empty space is doubtless related to his interest in atmosphere, an effective starting point for the impressionism of Velázquez, in which forms tend to escape from any restricting sharpness of outline and groups are no longer defined by distinct limits and separated into categories. The tendency was to express plasticity by means of focal points of light and aureoles.

In this universe of voids, of space, air and light, Velázquez appears to have singled out the hand as a symbolic image of the human being. In the *Old Woman Frying Eggs* the hands stand out and go to form a diagonal of action and reaction in a setting of passive and unmoving objects—a sharp active hand raised, a quiet passive one below. A similar play of hands occurs in the *Water Carrier of Seville*, marking a contrast between the boy actively grasping the glass, with its sharp, crystal-clear tonality, and the old man beside him, passively resting his hand on the clay jar, with its dull, opaque tonality. A luminous hand is the center of the icons composed in deep shadow as well as of the triangular central void in the *Adoration of the Kings*, thus expressing the generosity of the offering; and the same symbol is present in *St Ildefonso receiving the Chasuble from the Virgin*.

Hands lifted in the air determine the main lines of force in the mythological compositions, and in the *Surrender of Breda* a hand marks the center of the picture. If in the *Maids of Honor* we witness what might almost be called a ballet of hands, in the *Tapestry Weavers* nearly all of them are concealed and this gives predominant importance to the dark hand of the woman spinner. The *Rokeby Venus* has no hands. This is her whole essence. A rare nude in Spanish art, she is denuded of that which in all other works is symbolized by hands. In the splendor of her physical presence, coupled as it is with a direct allusion to the void, the illusory void of the mirror, she seems the clearest embodiment of the ultimate meaning of the art of Velázquez—a meaning to be sought for in the persistence with which, in picture after picture, he draws a deliberate comparison between illusion and reality.